A WOMAN'S KABBALAH

A WOMAN'S KABBALAH

Kabbalah for the 21st Century

VIVIANNE CROWLEY

Thorsons

Thorsons
An Imprint of HarperCollins*Publishers*
77–85 Fulham Palace Road
Hammersmith, London W6 8JB

The Thorsons website address is: www.thorsons.com

Published by Thorsons 2000

1 3 5 7 9 10 8 6 4 2

© Vivianne Crowley 2000

Vivianne Crowley asserts the moral right
to be identified as the author of this work

A catalogue record for this book
is available from the British Library

ISBN 0 7225 3879 0

Text illustrations by PCA Design

Printed and bound in Great Britain by
Woolnough Bookbinding Ltd, Irthlingborough, Northamptonshire

CONTENTS

ACKNOWLEDGEMENTS

This book is the result of the Wisdom and Understanding of many over the years – of Gabriel and of others who have taught me, and of Chris and those with whom I have walked the sacred paths. And with many thanks as always to the Centre for Transpersonal Psychology for their continual inspiration.

INTRODUCTION

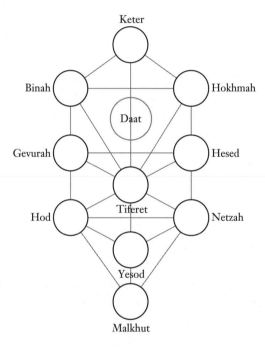

Keter

Binah

Hokhmah

Daat

Gevurah

Hesed

Tiferet

Hod

Netzah

Yesod

Malkhut

WHAT IS KABBALAH

Kabbalah was brought to the West by Jewish scholars and mystics. It remains an esoteric tradition within contemporary Judaism, particularly amongst the Hasidim. The Hasidim are the 'devotees' or 'pious ones' whose movement arose in 18th-century Eastern Europe just as a rationalist current in Judaism was pushing Kabbalah underground. Kabbalah is also one of the foundations of the Western Mystery Tradition, the body of esoteric teaching drawing on ancient Greek Neoplatonist philosophy, Chaldean astrology, Jewish Kabbalah and the Egyptian Mysteries, that has given rise to modern astrology, divination systems such as the tarot, ritual magic as a system of personal and spiritual development, and Goddess spirituality such as Wicca.

The Hebrew word Kabbalah derives from the word *Qibel* – to receive. This implies an oral tradition, transmitted by a personal teacher. Kabbalah, like many spiritual traditions, had information that was too sacred – or too heretical – to be written down. Kabbalah is a mystical branch of Judaism. It is concerned with interpreting the secret inner meaning of sacred Jewish texts. It is also a method of spiritual development to reach advanced states of consciousness that bring us closer to the Divine. These states are empowering. Kabbalah is a philosophical system. It helps us understand our place in the cosmos. It tells us why we exist, why we are born, why we live, the purpose of our lives, and where we are going when we complete our current cycle of incarnation.

ENCOUNTERING KABBALAH

My first knowledge of Kabbalah came from reading books, but I knew it only as a tradition for men. It was not until my late teens that I came to another understanding of Kabbalah. I was working, before going to university, for the psychologist Sam Smith, a member of the Board of Deputies, the representational body of British Judaism, and living in one of London's Jewish heartlands, Stamford Hill, home of the Hasidim. I began to read the work of Dion Fortune, the outstanding female magus of the 20th-century Western Mystery Tradition.

One morning, I was reading Dion Fortune's book *The Mystical Qabalah* while travelling to work on the top deck of a bright red London bus – the number 73 from Stamford Hill to Victoria. A middle-aged woman sat down beside me, glanced over and saw what I was reading. I struck her as rather unusual. Teenage girls with waist length hennaed hair did not normally sit on buses reading books about Kabbalah. She struck up a conversation. By the time the bus reached Oxford Street, she had told me that she was the co-head of a Kabbalistic magical order and I had agreed to a meeting later that day.

At exactly 6pm I was to stand at the foot of the Duke of York's steps on the Mall, just down from Buckingham Palace. A large black car would stop, driven by a man called Gabriel. I was to get in the car and he would take me to a house in North London where I would meet members of a Kabbalistic ritual magic lodge. My left-brain told me that in a large city like London, this was a reckless thing to do and, by the way, didn't this sound a bit like the beginning of a horror novel? My right brain told me that the candle I had lit two weeks before to ask the Divine to send me a teacher had been answered. In total confidence, well almost, that my intuition was right, I waited at the bottom of the steps at the appointed time and got into the car. Six months later I was initiated into the lodge.

Since then Kabbalah has been a major influence in my life. The Kabbalah is a map of the universe. All our experiences, both spiritual and mundane, can be understood within its framework. For both women and men, I have found ritual and meditative work within the Kabbalistic tradition to be a path to personal insight and spiritual growth. My career has been as a psychologist, therapist and Lecturer in Psychology of Religion at the University of London. In psychology, I also encounter the Kabbalah. Sigmund Freud's psychoanalysis was strongly influenced by the Kabbalah. Many of the themes in his psychological theories and even his methods have Kabbalistic overtones. Kabbalah also influenced psychologist Carl Jung's ideas on archetypes and psychological growth. The after-death vision of the 17th-century Kabbalist Knorr von Rosenroth was read as part of Jung's funeral ceremony.

I have called this book *A Woman's Kabbalah* for the obvious reason that I am a woman. This colours my approach and viewpoint, which is also influenced by the practice most of my life of Wicca and Goddess spirituality. This does not mean that this book is for women only, but my life experience means that I interpret Kabbalah differently from a Jewish Rabbi or male Christian ritual magician. In particular, for me the world of the body and of Nature is as important as the world of spirit. Too often, the journey to the Divine is shown as a journey away from the world, a journey towards transcendence. For me, the journey to the Divine is also a journey into the world, a journey into immanence and into humankind's and Nature's deepest heart; for within each cell, molecule, atom, and particle of our universe is the indwelling spirit eternal of the ever-belovèd Divine.

WHERE DID KABBALAH COME FROM

Kabbalistic teaching derives mainly from three texts that survived into modern times – *Sefer Yetzirah* or *Book of Creation* (*c.* 300–600 CE),[1] *Sefer Bahir*, the *Brilliant Book* or *Book of Illumination*, first published in Provence in 1176, and the lengthy *Sefer Zohar* or *Book of Splendour*, which first appeared in Europe in the 13th century. The *Bahir* introduces the concepts of the ten sephirot or emanations of the Divine and of reincarnation. The *Sefer Yetzirah* is the first core work of Kabbalah. It claims to be the secret teachings of the Patriarch Abraham and is a meditative text designed to produce mystical insight. The *Sefer Zohar* explains Kabbalah's beginnings by weaving myth and historical fact. The Divine is said to have first taught the Kabbalah to a select group of angels. After the famous Garden of Eden incident, the angels taught the secrets to the first human – Adam. The teachings were passed to Noah of the Ark, then to the Jewish leader Abraham, who took them to Egypt where some of the teachings became known to the ancient Egyptians and spread to the East. Moses was initiated into the Kabbalah in Egypt. During the Israelites' forty-year wanderings in the wilderness, Moses spent his leisure time studying Kabbalah with the assistance of lessons from an angel. From Moses, the teachings were transmitted orally. King David and King Solomon were deeply initiated into Kabbalah.

The *Zohar* claims that no one dared write down the teachings until Rabbi Shimon son of Yochai, who lived at the time of the destruction of the second temple in 70 CE. Rabbi Shimon wandered the Galilee area as a mystic before hiding in a cave for twelve years, where he dictated the teachings to his disciple Rabbi Abba. After his death, his son Rabbi Eleazer, his secretary Rabbi Abba, and his disciples collated his teachings into the *Zohar* or *Book of Splendour*. The book was then hidden in a cave near Safed in Palestine. Now the story becomes not dissimilar to the more recent discovery of the Dead Sea Scrolls. Arabs found the scrolls and, not realizing their importance, used them as food packaging. A Kabbalist from Safed purchased some fish at a local Arab market and found it had been wrapped in an ancient text. He realized it was Kabbalistic and purchased all the paper the fish seller had. From these writings, the *Zohar* was reconstructed and published.

The text came to Spain where Rabbi Moses de Leon (1238–1305) published it, possibly assisted by other Kabbalistic scholars. Some ideas in the *Zohar* seem original to Moses de Leon and his colleagues. Others are of greater antiquity. As well as Jewish mysticism, there are traces of Pythagorean mathematics, Plato, Aristotle, Alexandrian Neoplatonists, Eastern and Egyptian Paganism, and early Gnosticism. Comparisons have been made between Kabbalah and other esoteric traditions such as the Sufis, Cathars, Tantra, the Hindu *Upanishads*, and Buddhism. The *Zohar* attempts to explain the historical problem of why other spiritual traditions share similar ideas to Kabbalah, by claiming that Kabbalah is an age-old tradition that influenced their development. An academic scholar might argue exactly the opposite. The famous Kabbalistic scholar Gershom Scholem (1897–1982), Professor of Jewish Mysticism at the Hebrew University in Jerusalem, believed that Moses de Leon was the author of the *Zohar*. This view is unpopular with traditional Kabbalists who are unwilling to expose sacred works to academic scrutiny, but Scholem cites persuasive evidence. The *Zohar* makes frequent errors in Aramaic grammar and there are traces of Spanish words and sentence patterns.

There is also an interesting story about Mrs de Leon.[2] In 1291, Muslims conquered the city of Acre in Israel and killed most of the Jewish and Christian inhabitants. A young Jewish scholar, Isaac son of Samuel, managed to escape to Italy and travelled to Spain. He was astonished to learn of the existence of the *Zohar*, which he had never heard of in Israel. He sought out Moses de Leon, whom he met in the town of Valladolid. Moses de Leon promised that he would show Isaac the original ancient copy of the book if Isaac would visit him at his home in Avila. Moses de Leon was never to reach Avila. He became ill on the way home and died. Isaac heard the news and went to Avila to see if he could see the manuscript. There he learned that the wife of Josef of Avila, the province's tax collector, had offered her son in marriage to the daughter of Moses de Leon in exchange for the original manuscript of the *Zohar*. Moses de Leon's wife said that there had never been an original manuscript; it was her late husband's own work. He had made up its ancient lineage so that people would value it. This does not totally disprove the *Zohar*'s ancient claims. Perhaps Moses de Leon's widow had already sold the manuscript and did not want to admit it. Perhaps she did not want to trade her daughter for it. However, the story raises doubts about whether the teachings really originated as early as claimed by Moses de Leon. Whatever its origins, Kabbalah is an important body of mystical work. It is likely that the *Zohar* was based on older oral teachings and it was common to ascribe ancient religious and magical texts to great persons of antiquity in order to give them more importance. There are also religious reasons why it would have been in Rabbi Moses de Leon's interest to pass off his own writings as having impeccable orthodox credentials. Kabbalah's speculations about the Divine differ significantly from Biblical revelation.

Kabbalah flourished in Spain but in a climate of increasing persecution of Jews by the Christian majority. In 1492, the year that Christopher Columbus set sail for America, his most Catholic majesty the King of Spain expelled all Jews from Spain on pain of death. Huge numbers of Jews fled, settling across Europe and bringing with them their knowledge of Kabbalah. Teaching about Kabbalah amongst non-Jews began to flourish. Kabbalistic texts were translated into European languages and the newly-invented printing presses meant that the translations could be read by large numbers of people. The climate was receptive to the new teachings. Kabbalah appealed particularly to Christianized Jews. They or their parents had often been forced into converting and Kabbalah was a bridge between Christianity and Judaism. Kabbalah also appealed to non-Jews. From the 15th century onwards, Europe saw a Humanist Renaissance that revived interest in the Pagan traditions of Greece, Rome and Egypt, and in esoteric teachings and lore. The meeting of Kabbalah with European thought gave birth to the Western Mystery Tradition. This produced ritual magic groups such as the Rosicrucians and later the Golden Dawn. Kabbalah also strongly influenced the development of Goddess spirituality and Wicca.

THE TREE OF LIFE

Important in Kabbalah is the symbol of the *Etz Haim*, the Tree of Life. The Tree of Life represents the totality of creation – all that was, is and will ever be. Why a Tree? Many ancient spiritual traditions used a tree to symbolize the cosmos. Trees are evocative. They are the tallest of the plant and animal kingdoms. They can live the longest; most species will outlive a human being. Trees give us a sense of age, permanence and stability. They are rooted deeply in the earth, but rise to the heavens. They provide shade and shelter, and fallen branches to make fire. Trees have always seemed friends to humankind and, of course, our far ancestors the apes inhabited them. Deep within the human psyche is the image of the Tree as the point of origin.

The totality of creation represented by the Tree of Life is separated into ten emanations or *sefirot*. The singular of *sefirot* is *sefirah*. The word first appeared in the *Sefer Yetzirah* or *Book of Creation*. It is based on the Hebrew word for counting. In the *Sefer Yetzirah*, the sefirot are seen as the principles behind number and as different stages of creation. Over the centuries, the concept evolved. In a later important text, *Sefer Bahir* or *Book of Illumination*, the sefirot are related to different qualities and activities of the Divine.

The names of the ten sefirot are most commonly given as:

1. Keter – Crown
2. Hokhmah – Wisdom
3. Binah – Understanding
4. Hesed – Love, or Gedulah – Greatness
5. Gevurah – Severity
6. Tiferet – Beauty or Harmony
7. Netzah – Victory or Endurance
8. Hod – Splendour or Glory
9. Yesod – Foundation; sometimes replaced by All
10. Malkhut – Sovereignty or Kingdom; sometimes replaced by Shekhinah

Between Binah and Hesed is a state of being known as Daat – Knowledge. This is not a sefirah as such but acts much like one. The names of the sefirot derive from Biblical text. For instance, in describing Betzalel's qualifications to be a helper of Moses the Divine is described in the Bible as saying:

> *I have filled him with the Spirit of God (Keter),*
> *with Wisdom,*
> *with Understanding,*
> *and with Knowledge.*
> EXODUS 31:3[3]

The next seven sefirot appear in the Bible in a prayer of praise by King David:

Yours, O God, are the Greatness (Hesed),
the Power (Gevurah),
the Beauty (Tiferet),
the Victory (Netzah),
and the Splendour (Hod),
for All (Yesod) in Heaven and Earth;
Yours, O God, is the Kingdom (Malkhut).
I CHRONICLES 29:11

The sefirot of the Tree of Life are arranged in three columns often called pillars. As you look at the Tree diagram, the column on your right is called the Pillar of Force and the column on your left is the Pillar of Form. They can be thought of as action and reaction. Between them is the central column, the Middle Pillar, the balance between these two extremes. The Pillar of Force is often associated with the element of Fire and the Pillar of Form with water. Air is the element of the Middle Pillar. The Pillar of Force is frequently associated with the masculine and the Pillar of Form with the Feminine. The Middle Pillar is where masculine and feminine meet.

THE PATHS OF THE TREE

The tree image is derived from that of a real tree, but over time it has evolved to be a diagrammatic representation of the sefirot as levels of reality that separate the human from the Divine. The sefirot are joined by different paths, *Netivot*. This is a word that occurs rarely in Hebrew texts and it is not used in the sense of ordinary paths that one walks along. *Netivot* are paths or ways that we must make for ourselves. The paths are hidden and await our discovery. They are not places but states of consciousness that are accompanied by particular spiritual realizations. Theoretical Kabbalah teaches the intellectual knowledge that can help us attain these states and find the hidden pathways, but intellectual knowledge alone will never give us spiritual experience. To experience these states, we must learn meditative, ritual and devotional techniques that engage the spirit and heart.

ABOUT THIS BOOK

This book is an introduction to Kabbalah for those of all backgrounds and faiths. It is not a book for the specialist, but a guide for those who wish to find within the Kabbalah a framework to help make sense of their life experiences and spiritual journey. Kabbalah is one of many traditions that can help us in our spiritual quest. For me, the Kabbalah is not a unique Divine revelation with a claim to special status, but one of many currents of thought that have influenced Western spirituality. The truths discovered by Kabbalists have been discovered in other spiritual traditions, particularly those of the East. However, Kabbalah has the advantage of being Western-based and nearer to our cultural heritage and categories of thought than those of Eastern traditions. Persecution of Jews in Europe has had a similar effect to persecution of Tibetans by the Chinese. Sacred traditions that were once the deeply-guarded secrets of a few have been disseminated into the wider world to enrich our spiritual and cultural heritage.

This book is both theoretical and practical. Each chapter contains explanations of the different *sefirot* or emanations of the *Etz Haim*, or Tree of Life, the Kabbalistic map of the spiritual universe. From this, we come to understand how each *sefirah* relates to our everyday lives. I explain how the sefirot manifest in separate but parallel dimensions – that of cosmic evolution, that of the unfolding of the qualities of the Divine, in terms of human development and in everyday life. Each chapter has exercises to help you explore this further. Some exercises look at how different Kabbalistic energies can be found operating within our own lives. Other exercises are to help us understand how these energies manifest in the spiritual realm. Often you will be asked to work with imagery, because Kabbalah uses symbol and analogy to help us understand its teachings. Some exercises are practical; some involve quiet meditation or visualization. For some you will need to write and for others you will need to paint or draw. The idea of painting or drawing will alarm some people. 'I can't draw,' is a common cry, but 'can't' is a limiting word that prevents us using all of ourselves. 'Can't' usually means, 'I find it difficult.' However, those things we find difficult are often those from which we learn the most. The point here is not artistic merit; but creative exploration of the different themes and ideas.

At the end of each chapter, I give some characteristics and symbols that are associated with each sefirah. These include the Divine Names in Hebrew and deities from other spiritual traditions that correspond to the idea or energy of the sefirah. Kabbalistic text gives us numerous titles and images for the various sefirot. All these are ways to help us understand the sefirot better. The sefirot are also associated both in the early Kabbalistic texts and in the Western Mystery Tradition with cosmic phenomena such as the planets. There are differences in the attributions given by different authorities. Kabbalistic source texts give various colours for the sefirot. Unfortunately, the *Zohar*, *Bahir*, etc, do not all agree. Tiferet, for instance, is described variously as yellow, purple or green. Rather than give all the various alternatives, I have given the colours and planetary attributions used in ritual magic by the Western Mystery Tradition. These colours I know work well for those of a Western background. They are based on our psychological response to colour as developed through culture and art. In the Western Mystery Tradition, each sefirah has a main colour that is used for meditation and visualization. There are also some subsidiary colours. I mention the subsidiary colours where they are useful to know.

There are various correspondences in Kabbalistic texts such as the *Sefer Yetzirah*, *Zohar* and *Bahir* between parts of the human body, parts of a human image of the Divine, and the different sefirot. They do not all agree. In the *Bahir*, for instance, Gevurah is associated with the left hand of God. The Western Mystery Tradition associates the right hand of the human body with Gevurah. Often the feminine was associated with the left hand and some of the differences in attribution may be attempts to associate what are considered 'feminine' sefirot, such as Gevurah, with the left side of the tree. In this book, for the human body I have used mainly the attributions of the Western Mystery Tradition, which are based on visualizing a human being standing with his or her back to a diagram of the Tree of Life. These relate well to other spiritual systems such as the Hindu chakra system and are more logical than some of the early Kabbalistic texts.

Kabbalah is rooted in Jewish tradition, but you do not have to be Jewish to understand the basics of Kabbalah. If you wish to read the original texts, many are translated into modern languages. There are aspects of Kabbalah that are inaccessible unless you have a thorough grounding in Hebrew, but these need not concern us here. At the end of this book, I offer suggestions for further study for those interested in both Jewish and Western Mystery Tradition Kabbalah.

A WORD ABOUT LANGUAGE

As you will notice, there are many different spellings of Kabbalistic terms. In English, Kabbalah can be written as Qabalah, Cabbala and variations of these. Complications arise because originally Hebrew did not have written vowels and Hebrew has some sounds that do not correspond to Standard English. For instance, the word Hokhmah, Wisdom, can also be written 'Chokhmah'. This is because its first letter is pronounced like 'ch' in the Scottish word 'loch', or German 'ch'. Just to complicate things further, although Hebrew is becoming more standardized, Jews from different parts of the world have pronounced it differently. Imagine a Japanese, an Italian and a German speaking English and you will get the idea. If you read other books about Kabbalah, you will find that the final emanation on the Tree of Life, Malkhut, can be written as *Malkus* or *Malkuth*. This is because the final letter of the word, which is the Hebrew Tau (also written Tav), is pronounced like 's' by northern European Ashkenazic Jews, as 't' by southern European Sefardic Jews, and as 'th' as in 'thing' by non-European Sefardic Jews. Other complications arise because in Hebrew some letters are pronounced differently depending on where they appear in a word. P (Peh) is pronounced 'p' at the beginning of a word and 'f' in the middle. If languages are not your strong point, do not despair. Here I keep as much as possible to spelling that translates the Sefardic pronunciation into forms that can be most easily understood by speakers of English. This means that I use spelling that is more like modern Jewish Kabbalistic texts than the books of the Western Mystery Tradition, which use aesthetically pleasing, but more complex spelling.

EXERCISES

Each chapter in this book tells you something about the sefirah it describes. We can absorb this information using our rational minds, but we can better understand the nature of the sefirah if we try in some way to experience it and to relate it to our own lives. The exercises are designed to let you gain a deeper and more intuitive insight into what the sefirah represents in your own life.

In exploring the sefirot through these exercises, you are often asked to use visualization and imagery. The idea that we can explore deep within us using imagery and meditation will be familiar to many people, but if you have not tried this before, using imagery is a very powerful way of getting in touch with feelings and insights that lie hidden in our unconscious. Most of the exercises suggest that you record your experiences and insights by writing or drawing. You might like to set aside a book or file for your notes. Record the day and time that you do each exercise. You may find that certain times of day are better for you than others. Ideally you do not want to be too tired and you do want to be relaxed. When you reach the end of this book, you can look back at your exercise notes and review the insights you have gained.

A FIRST EXERCISE: THE TREE OF LIFE IN EVERYDAY LIFE

This is a simple meditative exercise. Sit down in a quiet room with dim lighting. Sit up in a chair or in a meditative position that you find comfortable. Now close your eyes and imagine the following scenario. Try tailoring the visualization as closely as possible to your own life.

0. Imagine yourself in bed asleep. You exist but you are not in a state of consciousness awareness. This is an 'Ain' state.
1. You open your eyes. You wake into awareness. This is Keter. Before you were alive. Now you know that you are alive.
2. Your eyes focus and you see. This involves an interaction between self and other, you and your environment. You see that which is around you. This is the state of duality – Hokhmah, twoness. Your sensory

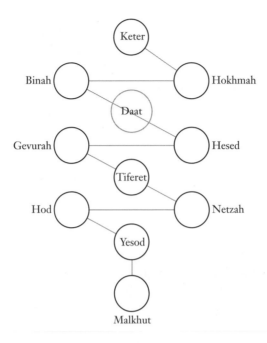

The Evolution of the Sefirot

apparatus scans the environment. You have seen it is daylight and that is time to get up. You have moved. You begin to stir from your night-time womb of the bed.

3. You stand up, still wobbly from sleep, and trip up. You fall down and hurt your knee. You sit back on the edge of the bed again. Your first attempt did not quite work, but the fall and the pain have woken you up a bit more. You have processed information and understood it. This is Binah. This time you stand up successfully. The second attempt is not quite the same as the first. On your second attempt, you have the memory of the first occasion. You have Knowledge (Daat). The fall is in the past. It no longer exists, but the memory and knowledge of it shape the present and future. This is the hidden Knowledge of Daat.

4. It is a bright sunny day. You feel happy and full of plans – things to make and do. This is Hesed, a realm of abundance.

5. Suddenly you stop in your tracks. You realize that you cannot possibly do everything you plan. There isn't enough time. Doing one thing will preclude another. You must make choices. You are limited in terms of what it is possible to achieve. In fact the pain in your knee from the fall may have restricted you – for today at least. The choices are painful. You want to have it all, but you can't. You have experienced Gevurah. You select some activities and dismiss the rest as pipe dreams.

6. You weigh up the decisions: the path from Gevurah to Tiferet is ruled in the Western Mystery Tradition by the tarot card Justice and its scales. Perhaps your choice is based on the longer-term goals and ambitions that you have. You have an objective and you select and reject your day's activities based on what serves it. You also want to have some fun. You want balance and harmony in your life. You come to a satisfactory conclusion and feel pleased with yourself. You have experienced Balance and Harmony, Tiferet.

7. Your partner is in the kitchen. You go out to give him or her a cuddle. You experience a warm emotion. This is Netzah.

8. You sit at the breakfast table and read the morning newspaper. You turn to the pages of foreign news. Your country is involved in a war. 'How did we get into this situation?' you ask yourself. 'Why are we doing this? What can we hope to gain? Will our intervention help those people – or will it make things worse?' You try to make some logical sense of what is going on. You are experiencing Hod.

9. Your partner comes into the room looking very attractive. You are sexually aroused. You mind flits to a good-looking colleague in the office. You fantasize about what it would be like to make love to him or her instead of your partner. Exciting images go through your mind. You are experiencing Yesod.

10. Finally you go to the bathroom and then, hungry, begin to make breakfast. The needs of the body call. You have experienced Malkhut.

MOVING ON

Let us now pierce the veil of mystery and step into the Kabbalistic universe.

Notes

1 'CE' means 'Common Era', our Western dating system. Non-Christians use this instead of the Christian term 'AD' or *anno domini*, 'the Year of Our Lord'.
2 Daniel Chanan Matt ed (1983 pp3–4).
3 This is a translation from Hebrew into English. English translations often obscure the Kabbalistic links. Translations of the Bible are drawn primarily from Yang's Literal Translations from Hebrew and Greek.

THE REALMS OF
THE UNMANIFEST

In the vastness of the void,
before beginning began,
when matter was non-existent,
there were three conditions.
The first we call AIN,
the Negative or Pre-existent,
the second we call AIN SOF,
Limitless or Ceaseless Expansion,
and the third we call AIN SOF AUR,
Limitless or Ceaseless Light.
From the awakening of AIN SOF from eternal repose,
and the contraction of the Limitless Ceaseless Light
to create new space,
it all began.

THE DIVINE AND THE COSMOS

The first stage of the evolution and revelation of the cosmos began in the Divine. Before anything else existed – before time, space or matter – is the Divine. The first state of Divine existence we call Ain, Negative existence or Pre-existence, the second we call Ain Sof, Limitless or Ceaseless Expansion, and the third we call Ain Sof Aur, the Limitless or Ceaseless Light. Think of the Pre-existent Divine as a Divine mind that is not yet aware of Its own existence. It rests in a timeless and spaceless realm. Before time began It was, is, and will be. It is beyond time and space; beyond categorization or name. It only *is*. Often when mystics speak of the Divine, they describe the Divine in negative terms: it is not this, not that. They are trying to convey the idea of something that is beyond attributes, categories and qualities that are but the products of the limited human mind. Ain, Ain Sof and Ain Sof Aur are like states of cosmic consciousness; or a better term might be the cosmic unconscious. Ain, Ain Sof and Ain Sof Aur represent the Divine before It becomes aware of Itself. Many mythologies speak of an earlier form of unmanifest existence, before the universe as we know it. Scientists describe this as the period before the 'Big Bang'. From a single point came the 'Big Bang' – an explosion of force that produced the universe, its galaxies, planets and stars. This is akin to the coming-into-manifestation of the Divine from the realms of the unmanifest.

TITLES AND IMAGES

The Divine in Ain Sof is sometimes spoken of as 'Hidden God', 'Concealed One', 'Cause of Causes', 'Root of Roots', and 'That-which-thought-cannot-attain'. These titles try to convey the idea that we are dealing with the background or precursor to existence rather than existence itself. This is the Divine that is beyond our imagery or sensory experience. The nearest we can come to understanding this level of existence is to imagine something that is without boundaries – infinite, limitless, incapable of being measured, weighed or appraised. It is void beyond voids, being beyond being, light beyond light. We can get lost in superlatives and so lose our way. We must be content to know that we do not know and to contemplate the mystery.

THE QUEST FOR MEANING

The existence of Ain, Ain Sof and Ain Sof Aur has implications for our lives. There is a state of existence from which everything arises and to which all returns. So too, in our individual lives, there is a state of existence prior to our birth. We existed before we were born into this particular incarnation and we will continue to exist after we leave the physical plane. Our Earthly life is only one stage of our existence and one type of consciousness.

Why the repeated cycles of birth, death and rebirth? Is life just a meaningless wheel, or is there a higher purpose? Are there goals and destinies to which our lives aspire? Human life is composed of joy but also of difficulty, struggle and suffering. When life goes well, we are not necessarily concerned with the purpose of human existence. We have worldly goals to pursue. We strive to reach those goals – a good educational qualification, a partner, a nice home, children, a good job. Achieving them may satisfy us for a time, but what then? Are we satisfied? Do our needs cease? The answer, of course, is no. Human beings are endlessly seeking and striving. As we reach each new goal, we set our sights on another. This is positive. It is human curiosity, drive and striving that have enabled us to move forward, but they are also a curse. We are no longer animals satisfied when our needs for food, shelter, sex and companionship are met. We are plagued with existential questions about the meaning of life and death, suffering and joy. At difficult times of transition – as we enter adult life, when we have children, when children grow up, when relationships break down, and in illness or old age – the question of meaning reasserts itself.

The end of the 20th and the beginning of the 21st centuries have given people in Western society the time and means to seek answers to the deeper questions of life. When in past eras we were struggling on the edge of survival, and as our contemporaries in many countries still are today, then many spiritual questions were the prerogative of a chosen few. The ability today to pursue a spiritual quest has given birth to whole new spiritual movements and interest in holistic therapies. We experience shiatsu massage, we read the runes, we are regressed to our past lives, we sing our mantras, and we meditate daily. All these things can help us feel better about our lives, but they may not give us an underlying philosophy that can answer the questions our minds must inevitably ask. They can teach us simply to accept life the way it is and to adapt ourselves to it, without providing the answers we seek.

Another approach is to seek answers through science. This has helped us control the material world and has brought us a better standard of living. We have also developed a psychological science that has helped us to understand our own natures. However, neither science nor spirituality alone can help us understand our place in the cosmos and how we are to live our lives. Here we have need of a spiritual science.

Over hundreds, thousands of years, great minds have contemplated the existentialist questions we must all ask, and have wrestled with the complexities of the universe to find answers for us all. Kabbalah has been described as a mathematics of feelings. Kabbalah, like Buddhism, is an exact spiritual science. It has studied carefully how human beings think, perceive, aspire, love and search. It provides precise descriptions of every nuance of thought and feeling. It is an intellectual discipline that at the same time has made a profound study of the realm of feeling and spirituality. It teaches how we can use our feeling function to understand the complexities of the universe and how we can bring the mind into harmony with the spirit. Anyone picking up a book on Kabbalah will find mathematical and geometric diagrams. Kabbalistic training teaches people to think visually as well as intellectually and to create in symbol and image maps of the cosmos and of the human psyche. Perhaps this is why Kabbalists make good computer programmers and systems analysts.

STUDYING KABBALAH

Although Kabbalah is a logical system, mental gymnastics alone will not help us understand it. In order to understand the Kabbalah, we need to develop new levels of intuitive thinking, feeling and understanding. Kabbalah describes abstract states of being that are beyond our everyday sensate reality. Our sensory apparatus cannot help us understand the true nature of the cosmos, but through meditation, contemplation and the development of spiritual feeling we can come to an understanding of things that are beyond our everyday senses. In trying to understand the Kabbalah, we must attune ourselves to the Divine and invoke the Divine light of being into our hearts.

Often Kabbalists speak of 'allowing the light to correct us'. Imagine for a moment someone learning yoga for the first time. The student has a book but no Earthly teacher and asks for Divine help in learning this spiritual discipline. The Divine hears and responds. A column of light shoots down through the student's crown chakra. It is imageless but it conveys the intuitive sense of a straight alignment between Earth and Heaven. Instinctively our aspiring yoga student straightens her spine in order to align herself with the spiritual force she seeks. Similarly, when reading about Kabbalah, we can invoke the Divine light in order to understand what we study. In communing with Divine light in this way, the Divine light enters us. This is a pleasing feeling. When at the end of our meditation, we return to a normal state of consciousness, we remember what we felt and seek to retain as much of it as possible. Through practice, a change occurs in our inner being. We become more like the light we invoke. We develop a sixth spiritual sense, the spiritual vessel or *kli* that continues to exist even when the body dies. This light focuses first in the heart and then begins to expand and fill the whole being. We study Kabbalah to evolve both ourselves and humankind as a whole. As each person grows and develops, so the group soul of his or her generation evolves and takes humankind on a more evolved path.

One of the important teachings of Kabbalah is that if we have a true desire to seek the spiritual realm, then the spiritual realm will hear our call and answer us. We are not alone in the cosmos and the Divine will seek us, if we seek It. If it is our sincere aspiration to evolve, then gradually we feel a desire for spirituality. This process is called *segula* or 'remedy'. Those reading this book will already have begun their spiritual awakening, but for those who have not begun their spiritual quest, Kabbalah teaches that there is also hope. Those who do not attain their spiritual evolution in this incarnation will do so in another; until the Divine plan is fulfilled. Kabbalists teach that the Kabbalah is a means to help us change. In studying it we begin to alter within.

EXPLORING AIN

EXERCISE 1: MEDITATING ON THE INFINITE

This is an exercise to help you meditate on the infinite. We can try to capture the essence of Ain, Ain Sof and Ain Sof Aur in words, but we are going beyond a level where words are useful. Another approach is to work with images – although at this level we are also beyond images. However, images have the advantage of allowing us to access the unconscious rather than the logical conscious mind.

1. For this exercise, you will need some poster or watercolour paints; if you are an artist you may want to use more advanced materials. You will also need some plain white cardboard.
2. With everything ready, close your eyes and visualize yourself out in space surrounded by planets and stars. You are galaxies away, seeing stars that are far beyond anything you have seen on Earth. You are far away drifting at the beginning of time, at the beginning of the universe.
3. Now drift back further. You are drifting back to a time before time, and a state of existence before the universe was created. You are going back to when all was potential that had not yet taken shape or form. There are three aspects to this pre-existence – Ain, Ain Sof and Ain Sof Aur. Now take colours that seem right to you and paint shapes, symbols, or patterns of colour that can represent to you this time before time. Do not allow your conscious mind to interfere. Just let your hand take you across the paper as it wills. Say in your mind the words, 'Ain, the Negative Existence or Pre-existence; Ain Sof, Limitless or Ceaseless Expansion, and Ain Sof Aur, Limitless or Ceaseless Light,' as you allow your hand to work.
4. Keep the painting that results and pin it or prop it up in a place where you can see it when you read more about Kabbalah. In your painting you have a representation of the origin of things. This will help you by reminding you of the simplicity behind the apparent complexity that unfolds.

EXERCISE 2: BEFORE I WAS BORN – AN INNER JOURNEY TO CONTACT OUR PRE-BIRTH SELVES.

This is an exercise to explore our own personal 'Ain'. We emerge out of the darkness of the womb, but even before we come into the world there are influences that impinge upon us and begin to form our personalities. What are these influences? Firstly, there is ancestry: the genetic pool of ancestors who have passed on characteristics that influence our personalities. Secondly, there is the environment in which we are conceived and subsequently nurtured in the womb.

Looking at ancestry, what do you know of your past? Today, many families are split up across countries and between countries. We may not have contact with our birth parents, grandparents or great grandparents. Yet these people who existed before us helped form us. Making contact with our cultural inheritance can be important for understanding who and what we are and what influences us. Our ancestors' backgrounds have unconscious effects on us. If they were persecuted or refugees, they may have transmitted the traumas of these experiences down the generations. They may have passed on expectations of failure and persecution. Conversely, if they were people of power and influence, they may have transmitted other expectations down the generations – that we must achieve what others expect of us. Have we been taught lessons of social success or failure in the womb, even we before we began our own lives?

See now if you can begin to penetrate the veils of negative existence of your own being by making a genealogical tree of your family. Unless your family has already done a lot of research on its family tree, it may take a few weeks.

1. This is a research exercise for which you will need a large piece of drawing paper. You will also need pens, ruler, scissors and glue. If this is beginning to sound like kindergarten, don't worry. Ain, Ain Sof and Ain Sof Aur are the kindergarten of the cosmos. Remember kindergarten can be fun.
2. In a horizontal row near the bottom of the piece of paper, write down in order of birth your own name and the names of any brothers or sis-

ters you may have. Write the full names, dates and places of birth and death, if applicable. Above the names, see if you can find small photographs of each of you. Stick these above the names.

3. In the row above write the names and dates and places of birth of your parents. If your siblings had different parents, put these in too. Now see if you can find or obtain photographs of your parents at around the age that they were when you were born.

4. Next do some investigatory work through family and, if necessary, genealogical archives. Find out your grandparents' dates and places of birth. Work out how old they were when they gave birth to your parents, and try to obtain photographs of them at about that age.

5. Now go one generation further back to your great grandparents. At this generation you will have eight ancestors, whose genetic make up and experiences gave rise eventually to you. Write down their dates and places of birth. Paste on copies of their photographs if you can obtain any.

6. Write in the nationality, ethnicity and religion of your different ancestors, and their occupations if you can find these. Now you are beginning to create a map of fourteen human lives whose streams run like tributaries into the river of your own life.

7. When you have completed your four-generation family tree as much as you can, sit down and ask yourself these questions:

- What cultural, ethnic and religious traditions have I inherited? What cultural, ethnic and religious customs have my ancestors passed on? Have I explored these fully? Could I read about them, or perhaps visit places associated with them?

- What else have I inherited from my ancestors? Have I visited their places of birth? Could I do this on my vacations?

- What life patterns have I inherited? Have I been programmed to believe I can achieve everything, that I must achieve everything, or conversely that I am limited – that 'people like us' can't succeed, of that 'we don't do that kind of thing'? Were there certain expecta tions in my family about how women or men would behave and how they would live their lives? Have I followed these models and patterns or have I forged a different path? If my path is different, how has my family reacted – with support and love, or with fear and disapproval?

- How can I acknowledge the positive things that my ancestors have taught me? How can the lessons of their lives teach me something today? If there are people of courage in my ancestry, how can I emulate them in my everyday life? If there have been patterns of failure, what can I do in order to create a new pattern for the future?

There are no easy answers to these questions but if you ponder on them, you will begin to understand how we inherit potentials and patterns, which can influence our lives down the generations. Even before we began, before the manifestation of our personal Keter, previous levels of existence were influencing what we would become.

TO OUR ORIGIN

Let us turn now to the beginning of ourselves, to Keter.

I

KETER - CROWN

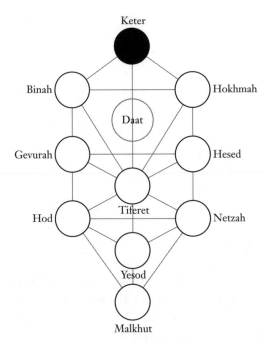

The first path is called 'Mystical Consciousness' (Sekhel Mufla).
It is the light that conveys understanding
of the Beginning that has no beginning.
It is the First Splendour.
No created being can attain to its essence.
SEFER YETZIRAH[1]

In the *Zohar*, the creation myth is a drama in which the Divine is revealed to Itself. It becomes aware of Its powers and attributes. Keter is the first emanation of the Divine. Before and beyond the Divine in Keter is Ain Sof Aur, 'Limitless light'. Beyond this is Ain Sof, 'Limitless or Ceaseless Expansion' and beyond this is Ain, Negative Existence or Pre-existence. Ain Sof Aur, Limitless Light, is beyond time and space. It fills everything and everywhere – except that there is no 'where' and no 'thing'.

ONE GOD OR ALL GOD

There are two similar but subtly different explanations of how Keter proceeds from Ain Sof Aur. One is that a movement arises in the Limitless Light, which concentrates around a centre. This centre becomes the first emanation, Keter, the Crown. From Keter emanates all of creation – human, animal, vegetable and mineral. This means that the Divine formed the cosmos out of its own substance and that the Divine is immanent or dwelling within creation. This is pantheism and fine for a Pagan. In fact, early Kabbalah was greatly influenced by Pagan Neoplatonist Greek Philosophy. Pantheism is anathema for monotheists, such as orthodox Jews, Christians and Muslims, who believe in a single perfect unchanging creator God who exists outside time and space.

To get around this problem, Rabbi Isaac Luria (1534–1572), who was head of the Safed School of Kabbalah in Palestine, explained the beginning of things in another way. Before everything was created, the Supernal Light of the Divine filled everything. There was no empty space. In order to begin creation, the Divine withdrew Its light from a circular space. A vacuum was created. A single thread of the Infinite Light extended itself into the void to form our cosmos. This was the beginning. Luria's idea of 'self-constriction' of the light of the Divine is called *Tzimtzum*.[2] It takes us into what is called *panentheism*, which can be compatible with monotheism or Paganism. The Divine is within creation – but also pre-exists it and will endure when this phase of material creation comes to its natural end. In fact, the idea is quite logical and matches the perception of many mystics.

CREATION AND COSMOLOG

In the beginning,[3]
when the King began to exercise his will,
he carved out signs from the Supernal Light.
A dark flame emerged out of the Concealed of Concealed,
the Mystery of the Infinite,
a formless vapour, set in a ring,
not white, not black, not red, not green,
no colour at all.
ZOHAR[4]

One of the primary concerns of Kabbalah is to explain the origin of the universe and our place within it. Kabbalah's mystical speculations are in poetic language that is quaint and archaic. What is interesting is how close they are to modern scientific ideas. If updated into modern language, the processes Kabbalah describes reveal a pattern similar to what scientists call the 'Inflationary Model' of the origin of the cosmos. Ain Sof, 'Limitless or Ceaseless Expansion', is symbolic of the Divine's infinite potential to create. It can be likened to what cosmologists call 'eternal inflation'; the infinite bubbling potential from which the universe arose before the 'Big Bang'. Keter represents the bursting through of the universe from the realm of pure potential to actual existence – the initial blinding instant of the Big Bang itself. To use more symbolic language, the awakening to consciousness of the Divine Pre-existent One (Ain) creates expansion (Ain Sof) and sends out Limitless Light (Ain Sof Aur). The Limitless Light concentrates a centre – Keter. From Keter, nine other emanations unfold one from another. To symbolize these, we could think of concentric circles, ripples in a pool, or the more conventional image of the Tree of Life at the top of this chapter.

THE DIVINE IN KETER

In the past, complex Pagan societies such as ancient Rome tried to accommodate their multi-racial and multi-cultural citizens by honouring every deity they could find, but generally cultures focus on only some of the many aspects of the Divine. Different spiritual paths focus more on the energies represented by some sefirot than others.

For cultural reasons, Judaism and Christianity have spoken of the Divine as male, but Keter is beyond male and female, which are only human constructs. Keter *is*. This has important implications for women. In Keter, the Divine is pure awareness, but it has no other attributes. Keter is the point when the Divine becomes conscious. It is not yet conscious *of* anything, because nothing else exists. However, the Divine is aware that It exists. Conscious awareness begins what can be symbolized as a thought process in the mind of the Divine. The Divine becomes aware of Its own existence and thinks, 'I am'. In Hebrew, *Eheyeh*, 'I am' or *Eheyeh Asher Eheyeh*, 'I am that I am', is the name of the Divine in Keter. This is the name that Moses learns when he asks the Divine in *Exodus* 3:14, 'What is your name?'

Keter is the realm where all is potential but nothing is yet realized. Nothing is separate from its origin. In the womb of the universe, the Divine has Its first conscious thought. It becomes aware of Its existence. This is the quickening.

TITLES AND IMAGES

In the Tree of Life, the nature of the Divine in each sefirah is hinted at in ancient titles for the sefirot found in Kabbalistic texts. In addition, non-Jewish students of the Kabbalah have related Pagan deities and Christian images to the different sefirot. These deities represent different personalities or incarnations of the Divine. There are also archetypal images associated with each sefirah. These give us other clues as to the nature of the Divine in the sefirah and the qualities of the sefirah itself. Keter's ancient titles include Ancient of Days, Greater Face, White Head, Existence of Existences, Smooth Point, and Most High. The titles are designed to convey the idea that Keter is the oldest and the first.

In Keter the Divine is unity. Keter represents all the different aspects of the Divine reconciled as one. Keter can be symbolized as whiteness, brilliance, or as the thousand-petalled lotus that surrounds the head of Buddha, which is white but represents all the colours of the universe. The image of a face seen in profile is sometimes used to represent Keter. This attempts to convey the idea that Keter is just emerging out of the unmanifest. One side of the face is turned back to Ain Sof. The other turns outwards to the universe It is about to create. Although this human image can be used, the nature of Keter cannot really be conveyed by the image of a personal human deity. In any event, Judaism, like Islam, prohibits making statues or pictures of the Gods and, in Christianity, the Protestant Reformation was keen to rid us of them. In fact, one of the commandments that Moses brought down from his encounter with the Divine on Mount Sinai was a ban on making statues or images of the Divine. The idea has mystical justification. Any representation of the Divine is limited to terms that we know – and the Divine exists beyond our human experience. The human mind is visual, however, and it is difficult for us to venerate what we cannot imagine. We tend to create images of the Divine based on our own life experience. A Jewish patriarchal nomadic society used terms such as 'Father' and 'Shepherd' to describe the Divine. Once we start to use such words, our minds associate them with visual images, even if we do not depict them outwardly. These visual images can be limiting. They can make it easier for some people to relate to the Divine than others.

One solution, difficult to make work in practice, is to ban images entirely. Another solution is the polytheistic one of allowing many different images of the Gods, which together make up a whole. This is the solution favoured by Hinduism and Western Paganism. Oneness and diversity can be reconciled. If we see the Divine emanations or different deities as different facets of a shining diamond, each of which reflects light slightly differently, we can reconcile Oneness with plurality. Using this image, Keter is the diamond and the other sefirot are its facets. The words 'reflect light' are important. They convey that even the exalted state of consciousness that is Keter is only a reflection of the Limitless Light of Ain Sof Aur.

There are advantages in spiritual systems that allow the Divine to be portrayed in many different ways for different people. The possibility of plural and equally valid images of the Divine leads us to an interesting idea

– that the Divine can be seen as male and female, gendered and androgynous, or as neuter. Of course the Divine is all and none of these things, but these multi-faceted images found in Kabbalah are illuminating. They mean that the Divine can be worshipped as Goddess as well as God. This is important if the Divine is to be accessible to all of us. Despite its image as a male-only spiritual tradition, the famous Rabbi Isaac Luria taught that. Kabbalah is for women and men.

KETER AND INDIVIDUAL DEVELOPMENT

In our own lives, Keter is equivalent to the foetus in the womb. It becomes aware of its own existence. It is still part of its mother, but it has come to life. The process of birth inevitably follows. At the end of our series of incarnations, we come back to Keter. We lose our separateness again. We are reunited with the original source and return to the womb of oneness. Our bodies die and are reunited with our Mother the Earth. Our spirits are reunited with the Divine Mother–Father of All, the Creating One of the Universe. Those who are great mystics may have brief periods where they experience union with the Divine, but full union with the Divine is a one-way journey. We can gain intimations of it through our meditations and spiritual life in incarnation but ultimate union, or re-union as it might be better termed, must be left to explore when we are beyond the veil of death.

SPIRITUAL EXPERIENCE OF KETER

Each of the sefirot is associated with a particular type of spiritual experience. Modern research shows that spiritual experiences occur to more than half the population but often people do not know how to express them or what these experiences mean. When we lived in homogeneous societies where everyone belonged to the same religious tradition, spiritual experience was easier to interpret. If our experience was expressed in orthodox symbolism and language, it was likely to be valued by our community. We might develop a reputation for holiness and acquire status. If our experience was unorthodox or challenged the views or authority of our spiritual leaders, then of course our fate was likely to be very different.

The spiritual experience associated with Keter is known as 'Union with the Divine'. There is no return from this experience, which takes us beyond the veil of death. Once we enter Divine Oneness, we become at one with Divine consciousness. Our individual lives are no more and we dissolve into the Divine. This state cannot be fully described because it is beyond words. It is a state of cosmic consciousness where the universe and we become one. There is neither subject nor object, I or other. I and other are One.

VIRTUES AND VICES

In the Western Mystery Tradition, the 'virtue' of Keter is said to be attainment. Keter has no vice. None of us is likely to experience attainment just yet, but the 'virtues' and 'vices' of the sefirot become important further down the Tree. Contact with a particular sefirah can manifest within us qualities associated with that sefirah. These can be positive or negative. What are virtues and vices? Virtues and vices can be better understood as different qualities, which manifest in our behaviour, attitudes, thoughts and feelings. If we experience the energy of a sefirah in our lives, it will have a certain impact on us. If we react to that energy in the wrong way, we experience unpleasant states of being. These are the vices. If we receive the energy correctly, then we experience pleasant and enlightening states of being. These are the virtues. Below the level of Keter, each sefirah is associated with many states of consciousness. The famous Kabbalist and legendary author of the *Zohar*, Rabbi Shimon son of Yochai, is reputed to have experienced all 125 states of consciousness available to human beings in incarnation; including an advanced state called 'Eliyahu the Prophet', in which the Prophet Elijah himself came to teach him. Here Kabbalah is similar to Buddhism. Tibetan Lama Anagarika Gorinda, for instance, describes 121 classes of consciousness that can be root causes of human action.

EXPLORING KETER

EXERCISE 1: I AM

This is an exercise to help you understand Keter's state of being of consciousness without qualities. It involves saying an affirmation.

I have a body, but I am not my body.
I have feelings, but I am not my feelings.
I have fears, but I am not my fears.
I have hopes, but I am not my hopes.
I have thoughts, but I am not my thoughts.
I have anxieties, but I am not my anxieties.
I have ideas, but I am not my ideas.
I have cravings, but I am not my cravings.
I have desires, but I am not my desires.
I am the One,
who perceives all these things,
yet is not these things.
I am I.
I was in the beginning,
I shall be in the end,
I shall be forever,
I shall be,
I am.

1. Write or type the affirmation in large print so you can read it easily.
2. Find a quiet time to do the exercise when you can sit in a dimly-lit room. You might like to light a candle. You could also play some soft music. Find a comfortable position to sit with your spine straight. You could sit on a straight-backed chair, you could sit cross-legged, or you could kneel in the 'Egyptian position' on your haunches if you are used to this.
3. Close your eyes and allow your breathing to become regular and even.

4. Open your eyes and read the first line of the affirmation. Become aware of your body. Now repeat the first line of the affirmation to yourself, either in your head or out loud.
5. Now go on and do the same for each line. Become aware of your body, feelings, thoughts and passions, each in turn, as you read and then say each line.
6. Rest for a while with the final line: 'I am.'

You can do this on a daily basis as a centring exercise. It is particularly helpful in times of stress, and when you have to prepare to make difficult decisions.

EXERCISE 2: 'WHO AM I'

For this exercise you will need quiet time alone in a dimly-lit room. Candle-light is helpful in setting the right relaxing mood. You could also play some soft music and perhaps burn some incense or perfume oil.

1. Close your eyes and relax. Imagine that you are going back in time. First of all you are yourself five years ago. Imagine how you were then.
2. Now go back five years more, and so on. At each five-year stage, visualize who you were then. It may help you if you think of the name by which you were known then. Many women change their last name through marriage or divorce. Your name may also have changed because of your mother's marriage or divorce. The personal name by which you were known may also have changed. Perhaps you had a pet name as a small child. Then perhaps you graduated to a new version of your name with your teenage identity, and so on. At each stage in your journey backwards in five-year stages, visualize how you looked and what you wore. Imagine your name being spoken in your mind.
3. When you come to toddler stage, try to remember your earliest memory. Now remember the context of that memory. Where were you living? What did your home look like? Who was living at home? Was your first memory pleasant or unpleasant, loving or not? These early memories may seem domestic or trivial, but they stay with us because

they give clues to the feeling tone of our life or they mark important stages in the development of our awareness.

4. Now think a little more about the environment in which you had your earliest beginnings. What did your parents tell you about your conception and birth? Were you a wanted child, or a careless mistake? Were you kept and loved by your family? Or were you given away or adopted? Was your entry into the world an occasion of joy – or of fear and foreboding? Were you the baby your parents wanted? Were you the sex they wanted? Were you physically perfect? Or was something not quite right? Were you the first child and therefore a new experience for your parents? Or were you born to an experienced parent? How old were your parents when you were born? Were they ready for parenthood, or did they think of you as a burden? Were you the first child in the family – or the first of your sex? Were expectations placed on you that your brothers and sisters did not have to cope with? What were these spoken or unspoken expectations?

5. You may feel that you do not know the answers to some of these questions, and it may be true that you do not consciously know. But do you know unconsciously? What do you feel are the answers to those questions, based on your earliest feelings, sensations and memories?

6. Take a piece of paper and write out these questions and your answers. Make a list of the expectations and note against them which ones you felt able to fulfil and which ones you did not. Have the expectations of others before you were even born damaged you or distorted your development in any way?

7. If we have good parenting, then we will be given a safe space in which to develop the best of ourselves, but not all parenting is carried out in safe space. Even well-meaning parents can create threatening, dangerous, strange, or unstable environments that mean that the seed within the child does not grow straight and true. Having made a list of the expectations that surrounded your birth, make a list of those that you would like to discard or change.

8. Remember that your life belongs to you. You are a unique individual and within you is the seed of the Divine from which you came. The Divine gives us all a purpose. Ask now that your particular purpose can be made manifest to you. You will not receive an answer straight

away, but your question creates a movement in the cosmos, an outward ripple that causes change that will eventually make the answer clear to you.

EXERCISE 3: PRAISE

A natural instinct within human beings is to honour that which gives rise to us, the source of our being. This is a Prayer of Praise that you can say whenever you wish to feel closer to the Divine. Moments of communion with the source of our being give refreshment to the spirit and strength to carry out our everyday responsibilities and tasks. If you learn this Prayer of Praise by heart, then you can say it silently to yourself anywhere you happen to be – at your desk, in your home, even on a busy commuter train.

Often spiritual exercises are surrounded by ritual. Simple acts such as lighting candles before we say a Prayer of Praise can help us focus more on what we are doing. They also help the moment seem more special. However, they are not essential. We do not have to be elaborate when we turn to the Divine.

Prayer of Praise

Holy art Thou, Creator[5] of the universe,
holy art Thou, whom Nature hath not formed,
holy art Thou, the Vast and the Mighty one,
Creator of the Light, and of the Darkness.

Holy art Thou,
beyond male and female, Thou art:
    Source of Life,
    Source of Wisdom,
    Source of Understanding,
    Source of Knowledge,
    Source of Compassion
    Source of Power.
    Beauty of Beauty,

Bringer of Endurance,
may Thy wondrous Splendour,
be our Foundation,
Thou who art Sovereignty,
Blessed be Thou.

Holy art Thou, the Vast and the Mighty One,
holy art Thou, whom Nature hath not formed,
holy art Thou, Creator of the Universe,
who exists beyond Eternity and Infinity,
who participates in every state of being –
changing but unchanging;
who transforms and renews everything,
in whom nothing is lost.
Creator of the Light and of the Darkness.
Blessed be Thou.

ONWARDS – FROM SEED TO WISDOM

Keter is the seed that is the core you. It is different from what subsequent experiences have made you. From Keter we can gain a sense of the Divine Oneness that lies at the heart of all things. This Divine Oneness has a purpose for you. To discern that purpose you will need Hokhmah, Wisdom, the second sefirah of the Tree of Life.

Keter – The Crown

Titles: Arikh Anpin (Aramaic – Greater Countenance or Patient One), Ancient of Days, White Head, Concealed of the Concealed, Existence of Existences, Smooth Point, Highest Point, Keter Elyon – Supreme Crown, Avir Kadmon – Primal Ether
Image: A face seen in profile

Divine Aspect

Hebrew Divine Name: *Eheyeh* – I am, or *Eheyeh Asher Eheyeh* – I am that I am
Deities in other traditions: The first deity or manifestation of deity in all traditions
Spiritual Paths: Unification mysticism of all traditions

Correspondences in the Physical Universe

In the cosmos: Reshit ha Gilgalim – the first swirlings, the Big Bang
Colour in the Western Mystery Tradition: pure white, brilliant white
Number: 1

Correspondences in Humankind

Spiritual experience: Unity with the Divine
Positive quality: Attainment
In the human body: Crown of the head

Notes

1. Translations are based on Kaplan (1997 ed.), Poncé (1974) and Wynn Westcott (1975 ed.).
2. Also written *zimzum*.
3. A reference to Genesis 1:1.
4. From the *Zohar*. Based on Scholem (1963 ed., page 3), Matt (1983, page 49), and Kaplan (1989, page xxiii).
5. You could use 'Creatrix', the female version of the word, if you wish.

2

HOKHMAH – WISDOM

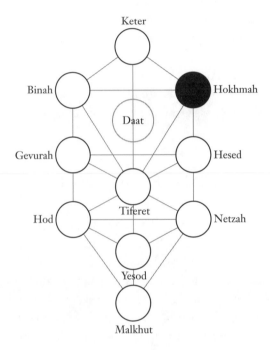

The second path is called 'Radiant Consciousness' (Sekhel Maz'hir).[1]
It is the Crown of Creation
and the splendour of the Supreme Unity,
to which it is most in proximity.
It is exalted above every head.
The Kabbalists call it 'Second Splendour'.
SEFER YETZIRAH

Hokhmah, Wisdom, is the second sefirah of the Tree of Life. It emerges from the first sefirah, Keter. If Keter is the Divine waking to awareness, Hokhmah is the Divine beginning to act. The Limitless Light of Ain Sof Aur concentrates a centre that is Keter. This centre creates a pressure. This wakes Keter to self-awareness. The thought 'I am' creates activity in Keter, the concentration of the Limitless Light. This activity becomes Hokhmah, an outward movement. Early Kabbalistic drawings sometimes tried to convey this by drawing the successive sefirot as concentric circles; rather like the ripples in a pool when a stone is thrown in.

If Keter is a focusing and crystallization of Divine Being into awareness, Hokhmah represents the activity of that consciousness. As soon as we become aware, we begin to question, desire and seek. We have the beginning of brain activity. All this is Hokhmah. The idea of movement, of the primal being reaching out and extending Itself into the cosmos is important in Hokhmah. Keter is awareness; Hokhmah is activity. Keter is being; Hokhmah is energy.

THE DIVINE IN HOKHMAH

The Hebrew Divine name in Hokhmah is Yah or Jah. This name appears mainly in Biblical Psalms. It is little used these days except by Rastafarians. Their beliefs are based on Ethiopian Christianity, an early form of Christianity that has had much interchange with the Falasha, or Ethiopian Jews. Yah is a male aspect of deity and Hokhmah is described as a masculine sefirah. It is often likened to an ejaculation of the Divine, which fills the next sefirah, Binah, the womb of the universe, after which creation begins.

Although traditionally Hokhmah is described as male, Wisdom is frequently described as 'She' in the Bible.

Happy are those that findeth Wisdom,
and those that getteth Understanding;
for its merchandise is better than the merchandise of silver,
and the gain thereof than fine gold.
She is more precious than rubies:

and none of the things that thou canst desire
are comparable unto her.
Length of days is in her right hand;
in her left hand are riches and honour.
Her ways are ways of pleasantness,
and all her paths are peace.
She is a Tree of Life to them that lay hold upon her:
and happy is everyone that retaineth her.
PROVERBS 3:13–18

Ideas about Hokhmah are also influenced by Greek Gnostic ideas of Sophia Goddess of Wisdom. Hokhmah is the second sefirah, where unity becomes duality. Hokhmah has both feminine and masculine aspects and is a foretaste of the fundamental duality of human biology – female and male.

THE COSMOS

Traditionally in the Western Mystery Tradition, Hokhmah is associated with the heavens and, more specifically, the twelve constellations of the zodiac. Our ancestors believed that our planet the Earth was the centre of the universe and that the stars and other planets revolved around it. The zodiac constellations seemed to them to be the outer limits of the circular universe that surrounded us. In modern day Kabbalah, we would associate Hokhmah with the chaotic beginning of physical and chemical reactions that gave rise to matter.

In the Western Mystery Tradition, Hokhmah is associated with those deities who are seen as rulers of the heavens and skies. In the ancient Egyptian religion, there is Nuit the Star Goddess who is depicted as stretched out over the night sky protecting the world beneath. Like Hokhmah, she is more like an abstract principle or energy than a personal deity. She is painted on the walls of tombs, but few statues are made of her. We have not yet fully entered into the world of form. This is also the realm of virgin Goddesses such as Athena, the Greek Goddess of Wisdom, who did not come into being via the womb of a Goddess, but sprang into existence from the forehead of her father Zeus. Athena, Wisdom, is the result of the thought of her father Zeus, here representing Keter. Athena emerges fully armed. She is also a fiery warrior.

TITLES AND IMAGES

Hokhmah's ancient titles include *Abba*, Father, and Hokhmah is sometimes referred to as the sefirah of the Supernal Father. The title 'Supernal Father' helps to convey the idea that Hokhmah is the beginning of activity and action in the cosmos. Keter, while the origin of deity, is somewhat more removed.

Keter is Unity and it can be represented as a circle. This is a shape formed from one line. In Hokhmah, the Oneness of Keter becomes Two. With duality we have the potential for shape but not yet for three-dimensional form. The shape of 'twoness' is the oval – a shape made by two interlocking curving lines. One image for Keter is of a face in profile; an image for Hokhmah is of a face full on. With Hokhmah, the Divine turns its energy outward. It looks out to see what it can see. At the level of Keter, the Divine exists alone. At the level of Hokhmah, the Divine has begun to change. There is duality – rest and movement. Another image used for Hokhmah conveys this duality. It is of a head with two faces.

> *Behold, Wisdom has two faces.*
> *The higher face turns toward the Crown (Keter),*
> *it does not gaze downwards but receives from above.*
> *The second face, the lower one,*
> *turns downward to control the sefirot,*
> *emanating of its wisdom to them.*
> TOMER DEVORAH[2]

A deity with two faces is an image found in other traditions. For instance, the Roman God Janus, who gives his name to January, the turning point of the year, has two faces. One face looks to the past and the other to the future. Hokhmah is positioned between Keter and that which is about to emanate from Keter – the manifest universe. If we think of the beginning of creation at this time, there is no form or substance, but energies have begun to interact with one another. This inter-action will create the cosmos.

Hebrew tradition speaks of a creation shaped by a male God, but the earliest creation myths spoke of a Creatrix, a creation Goddess. Often humans were unaware of the role played by the male in procreation. They thought of the Creatrix sometimes as a great bird who had laid a sacred egg from which hatched the cosmos. An egg is an ovoid, a shape connected with Hokhmah. Contemplate an image of an egg in your mind for a moment. Visualize it. Imagine holding a smooth egg in your hands. Imagine it first cold to the touch and then the warmth it would have if it came from straight beneath the warmth of its mother, the cosmic bird that gives birth to creation. What potential is here! Out of this fragile vessel comes forth life.

The Kabbalistic text *Sefer Bahir* relates Hokhmah to the eyes.[3] The oval shape of the eye is another image that conveys the 'twoness' of Hokhmah. The Divine is often spoken of in esoteric groups as the 'eye in the triangle'. This image comes from the first three sefirah of the Tree of Life. The dark pupil in the centre links us to the unmanifest, the Hidden God of Ain Sof. Keter is the circle, the iris. Around it is Hokhmah the oval of the eye shape and surrounding it is a three-sided figure, the triangle that is one of the symbols of the next sefirah, Binah. It is Binah that develops the basis for three-dimensional form.

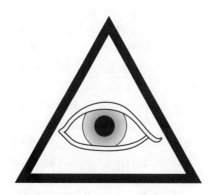

The Eye in the Triangle

RELATING TO GOD THE FATHER

Many children today do not have full-time fathers. Fathers may be absent completely. Their mothers may have a series of relationships, so children will have more than one father-type figure in their lives. Fathers are important for sons as role models. They are also important for daughters. Ideally, they give their daughters a sense of what it is to be valued as a woman and an understanding of the qualities of the masculine that will help women build relationships with men. When divorce, death or separation causes a disruption to the father–daughter relationship, or the relationship is abusive, something is lost. A girl who loses her father may have difficulty in relating to men without fear of losing them. She may feel insecure about her femininity and feel that no man will ever love and admire her. Sometimes an absent father is idolized and no real man can ever possibly match up to the perfect image.

For both sexes, if the relationship with the physical father is unsatisfactory or broken, a positive relationship with the masculine can be regained in other ways. One way is by forming a positive image of the masculine deity – the Father God. Unfortunately, the images that have developed of Father Gods in recent millennia have not always been positive ones. The Biblical God is often portrayed as vengeful, judgmental, angry – not a nice person to know. This image can be especially alienating for those who have suffered from inadequate or abusive fathering.

Hokhmah is the origin of our image of 'God the Father'. Sigmund Freud,[4] the founder of psychoanalysis, described himself as an 'Atheist Jew'. He believed that the Jewish and Christian God was nothing more than an exalted father figure. God did not create man in his image; man created God in his image. According to Freud, religious needs can be traced back to our infancy when we are helpless and dependent on adults. When in adulthood we are faced with insurmountable difficulties, we regress to our infant state. We long for a Heavenly Father who will take care of us and protect us from life's problems and realities.[5]

Freud suggested that the quality of the relationship with our physical father will affect how we perceive and relate to Father Gods. People with encouraging and supportive fathers are more likely to see God the Father as encouraging and supportive. People with angry or critical fathers would see the Father aspect of deity as angry and critical. Unlike some other species, human fathers are biologically programmed to play an active role in raising their children. In our modern complex societies, lack of social constraints means that many fathers abandon their responsibilities, but this does not change the biological programming. We have within us an archetypal image of what 'Father' should be. If there is no one to play that role, or it is played badly, then our relationship to the masculine will be damaged. We may find it difficult to relate to any form of masculine God. It also leaves us vulnerable to religious groups with charismatic male leaders who can appear to be the perfect father we have never known in real life. Many religious groups consciously or unconsciously exploit this. Psychologist Chana Ullman[6] studied the lives of 40 converts to Orthodox Judaism, Catholicism, Hare Krishna and Bahai. Compared to non-converts, the converts had experienced considerable family trauma involving extremely stressful relationships with absent or rejecting fathers. The new religious group was providing the love and nurture that the real father had never given.

HOKHMAH AND INDIVIDUAL DEVELOPMENT

In human development, Hokhmah equates to the process of birth. Keter represents becoming aware of one's own existence, 'I am'. This is a growing awareness that evolves during the nine months of gestation in the womb. Hokhmah is the next stage of awareness. If there is 'I', there may also be other or 'not I'. Hokhmah represents an outward movement into the universe. In Keter the unborn infant stirs and awakes. In Hokhmah the head engages and the infant begins her journey down the birth channel. She pushes outwards seeking the light of Binah. Hokhmah is the struggles of labour, until we emerge into the world. Our life journey and its struggle to assert our individuality and separate uniqueness have begun.

THE WISDOM OF THE FATHERS

Hokhmah is the second sefirah and is associated with duality. We encounter Wisdom at Hokhmah, but it is not our own. It comes from the world of the Fathers. Duality implies two possible standards of judgement – yours and mine. A danger of duality is that we adopt others' standards as our own. In the early stages of childhood that is exactly what is meant to happen. Our parents teach us certain behaviours, morals, values and standards of conduct. As infants our brains are malleable. This is necessary so that we can learn quickly the physical skills of walking and talking that we need to interact with the world. We are also malleable with respect to others' ideas. Psychologically we are not yet separate. We are within the parental space. Their ideas will be our ideas. Their language will be our language. We encounter wisdom in the form of the 'shoulds' and 'should nots' of our primary guardians – our mothers and fathers. At this stage, Wisdom comes from outside ourselves. We need not question this wisdom yet, but an important part of growing up is to make conscious what we have been told and to decide if we agree with it or not.

There may be much that we do not fully agree with, but have not fully questioned. In earlier times the framework in which the mother operated was circumscribed by the world of the fathers – the social and political establishment where women had no power. The mother was the primary influence on her children, but her worldview was formed by patriarchy, the world of the fathers. As newborn infants, we are suspended between the world of our parents and their past experience and the world of the future, which is as yet unknown to us. In our era in the West, we are going through rapid changes in male and female roles, but we are born still into a patriarchal world where men largely control the important institutions – government, commerce and religion. Generations yet unborn will emerge into a different world, but today our childhood expectations are shaped by a world dominated by men. This 'programming' is something both women and men may need to question.

SPIRITUAL EXPERIENCE
OF HOKHMAH

The spiritual experience of Hokhmah is the vision of the Divine face to face. At Hokhmah, we start to make human images of deity. Hokhmah represents the highest level of personal deity that we can conceive. Beyond Keter we have no concept of personhood, only of brilliant white light, the origin of all things. Not all religions have personal deities. Buddhism does not have personal Gods, although in some Buddhist traditions the veneration of the Buddha is like that paid to a God. However, in its purest form, the aim of Buddhism, like some forms of Hinduism, is to achieve a particular state of consciousness rather than to worship a personal deity.

HOKHMAH QUALITIES

The positive manifestation in the human psyche of the energy of Hokhmah is devotion. There is no vice. Hokhmah is like an unborn child, it is pure and unsullied, and in a state of innocence. We have not yet moved beyond the realm of pure energy and no Shadow side of Hokhmah can be conceived of by the human mind. Devotion is developed by worship of something – a personal deity or an idealistic cause. Devotion helps us to sacrifice the lesser for the greater and to lose our selfishness in the pursuit of something more important. This has been the object particularly of religions that venerate the Divine in human form rather than as an impersonal force. Religions that have personal deities offer to their followers, not unity with the object of their devotion, but eternal contemplation of it. Worshipper and worshipped remain separate and apart. The duality of Hokhmah is maintained. This is *devequet* or communion. This is the case with mainstream Judaism, Christianity and Islam. It is also the position that most orthodox Kabbalists have sought to retain. However, amongst the Hasidim, there have been teachers, such as the Maggid of Mezritch, who have taught *ahdut*, the *unio mystica*, the ultimate union of the soul with the Divine. Even if we start off as worshippers of a personal deity, mystical experience tends to change our notions about deity. Many mystical traditions within

Kabbalah lead their practitioners to the idea that the ultimate destiny of humankind is reunification with the Divine Oneness, which means that in the core of our being we carry something of the Divine.

Although we do not enter into full unity with the Divine until Keter, there is another type of joining that occurs at Hokhmah. Traditionally Kabbalah teaches that at Hokhmah we are all part of one human group soul. It is only at Binah, the next sefirah, that we assume our individual identity. At Binah we develop a *Neshamah*, or individual soul, also known as soul-breath or spiritual essence. We become undying spiritual beings whose origin is Divine and whose ultimate home at the end of all incarnation lies in or with the Divine. This has implications, of course, for the ultimate fate of humankind. If we are to return to one group soul, what implications does this have for our spiritual evolution and our relations with one another? If we all come from one source, one 'meta-soul', then we are all connected to one another. What one of us is capable of, good or bad, all of us are capable of. We have a collective responsibility for one another's actions. If we change our lives in a positive way we evolve the group soul. The reverse is also true. Our inner state of being, whether positive or negative, will affect those around us. Wisdom shows that it is our responsibility to evolve.

EXPLORING HOKHMAH

Here is a series of exercises to help you explore the role of Divine Wisdom and the image of the Father in your life.

EXERCISE 1: MEETING THE SUPERNAL FATHER

If your father experiences were not positive, this is not irredeemable. Within our psyche we all possess an image of the archetypal father. This archetype expresses itself in our images of Father Gods and of father figures in myth, film and novel. Arnold Schwarzenegger explored the father image in some of his films such as *Kindergarten Cop* and *Terminator 2*. He played the role of the father who is masculine and strong, but at the same time loving and protective, the father who would always be there for us. If our fathering has not been good, then we can help to overcome this by creating a strong link with the Father aspects of deity. Many sefirot are associated with father images. Hokhmah is the first of these. Here we explore the Divine Father as Heavenly Father of Hokhmah.

For this exercise you will need some large paper on which to draw, and some paints or coloured pens or crayons. You could write or type out the instructions in large print to read in dim lighting, or you could read them onto a tape. If you use a tape, allow gaps between each instruction for the visualization. Allow about an hour for the exercise. It should be done at a quiet time when you can be alone and undisturbed. It is best done in dim lighting that allows the unconscious mind a freer rein.

1. Imagine that you are on the green and grassy lower slopes of a mountain. It is a summer's day and the sun is warm above you. You are walking steadily upwards, following a well-trod path. The air is fresh and clean. The sky above you is blue and dotted with white clouds. You hear the singing of birds high in the air.

2. You climb for a long time. The birds are now far below you. The air grows colder, but you are well wrapped against the cold. The grass becomes sparse and the path more rocky. A mist descends. It blocks out the sky but the path shines clearly through the mist, leading you upward.

3. You make your way up the misty grey mountainside. Suddenly the mist begins to clear. You find you are just below the snow line. The sky is a cloudless blue and there is no sign of the sun. The mountain peak seems like a white island floating in a sea of cloud beneath a clear blue sky.

4. You find that the path ends just before the snow line in front of an ancient stone altar that has been weathered by the wind. You sit down on the smooth rock surface before the altar and rest for a while, your back against the altar. You feel the timeless peace of this place.

5. You place your hands on the smooth rock beneath you and find that near your left hand is an egg-shaped stone. You take the stone in your hand and you feel a sense of age, timelessness, strength, and power. It seems as though this mountain and the stone in your hand have stood

guard above the clouds for aeons and aeons.

6. Here you are at the sacred home of the ancient Gods. This is the sacred mountain of all peoples. Here the Father of Wisdom began and to here he will withdraw when this aeon of creation is complete. Contemplate for a while the nature of this deity who lives apart in the high places.

7. Now begin to ask yourself: what might the Divine Father do to help you and to give you wisdom and strength? The Divine may come as a voice, a breath, or a breeze. Let the breeze caress you and ask the Father of the Gods how you can better understand and appreciate the masculine and the men in your life – the fathers, sons, brothers, co-workers.

8. Ask the Heavenly Father of All to give you insights that you can take back down the mountain with you into the realm of your everyday life. Maybe words will come into your mind, or a symbol or image will come to you. Remember the words and images so that later you can record them.

9. When you have explored the words and images that come to you, you may have a question that you wish to ask the Heavenly Father about your own life's journey or about the masculine in your life. If so, ask it now.

10. Now focus on attuning yourself to Divine Wisdom. Here we are moving away from the Father God image created by humankind to the true essence that lies behind the image – the energy of Hokhmah. See if an image comes to your mind for Divine Wisdom. It may come in human form as Goddess or God, or as another symbol or image.

11. Now offer a prayer to draw Divine Wisdom into your life. Ask that that quality of Wisdom may manifest within you – in your feelings, thoughts, words and deeds. Ask that the power of Wisdom may guide you. This is something you could say. You may like to speak aloud.

Source of Wisdom,
Divine Parent,
sent forth from the beginning to make manifest the worlds,
cosmic flow of energy,
who gives life to the cosmos and to woman and man,

flow into my being,
allow me to commune with you,
so that in all that I do
I may manifest your timeless wisdom.

At the end say, 'Amen', or 'So Mote it Be'.

12. Commune for a while in the stillness, until you sense that the Divine presence is withdrawing itself. It is time to descend the mountain. You may take the egg-shaped stone with you if you wish, or you may leave it on the altar.
13. Before you leave, give thanks to the Divine presence in this sacred place and then descend once more through the mist, following the path until you emerge into sunlight and on grassy slopes once more. Then descend the pathway to the field below.
14. Find a patch of grass and sit down. In your own time, return to your everyday world.
15. Now draw the journey that you made – the mountain, path, cloud layer, altar, and the stone you found. Then write down the wisdom, insights, feelings and words that appeared to you on each stage of your journey.

EXERCISE 2: THE PERSONAL FATHER

Take some writing paper and a pen and write a heading 'My Father'. This is an exercise to explore your early relationship with your father. If you had a number of fathers in your life, then choose the one that most influenced your life from ages four to fourteen. Here are some questions to ask yourself. Write down the answers.

1. What is your earliest memory of your father's appearance and manner?
    - How old was he?
    - Was he attractive/unattractive?
    - What are the main characteristics that you remember?
    - What kind of interaction did you have with your father?

- Did you eat meals with him in the evenings – or did he or he and your mother eat alone?
- When you had meals together, were these happy occasions, or was there tension/anger?
- What was the source of the tension or anger?
- Did you father criticize your table manners or the foods you did or did not eat?
- Did you father prepare or help prepare meals or clear up? Or was this 'women's work'?

2. Did your father remember your birthday?
   - Did he buy you presents and cards?
   - Did he buy presents himself or did your mother do this for him?
   - Was giving gifts 'women's work'?
   - Did he promise you presents that he never bought?
   - Was he generous or stingy given your family income level? Or were presents too extravagant? Were presents a substitute for love?

3. Did your father visit his parents?
   - Did they seem important to him? Or was maintaining family con tacts your mother's responsibility?
   - Did he have close contact with brothers and/or sisters?
   - What did he convey about the importance of family and family responsibilities?

4. What was your father's religion?
   - Were you taken to religious services? If so, did your father attend or was religion something for women and children?
   - What images of womanhood were conveyed by the religion of your upbringing? Were women ministers? Were they in positions of responsibility and power? Or was your religion run by men? How did you feel about this? Did you ever question it? If so, what response did you get?
   - Did you ever change your religion and convert to another? Did you tell your father? If so, how did he react – positively or negatively? If you did not tell him, why not? What did you fear?

5. How did your father react to your social life?
   - Were your friends welcomed at home? Did your father express judgements about them, positive or negative? How did these make you feel?
   - Were you allowed to go out at the age when you felt ready? If you are female with brothers, were more restrictions placed on you than on them? Did your father encourage you to go out or did he prefer you to stay at home?

6. Did your father attend school functions?
   - Did he watch you perform in plays and/or sporting events?
   - Did he read your school reports? Was he encouraging, disinterested or critical? How did this make you feel?

7. Did your father comment on your appearance? What about your clothes? Were his comments positive or negative? How did this make you feel about your image?

8. What about boyfriends or girlfriends:
   - Did you tell your father about your first relationships, or did you hide them?
   - If you are female: were boys allowed to collect you from your home? How did your father react to your growing sexuality?

The different aspects of life that are covered by these questions are only some of the many ways in which your father will have impacted on you in your early years. His attitudes, both spoken and unspoken, will have influenced your ideas about what it is to be a woman or man, and about how women and men interact. He may also have conveyed, consciously or unconsciously, whether you met his standards of 'womanliness' or 'manliness'. This will have impacted on your sense of self-worth or of worthlessness. If you have absorbed negative attitudes, this does not mean that they cannot be changed. In beginning our spiritual quest, we begin a search for autonomy. First we must recognize who and what we are. The next step is to change it.

TO BINAH

We have walked to an encounter with Divine Wisdom. Let us now turn to Binah, Mother of the Cosmos.

Hokhmah – Wisdom

Titles: Abba – the Supernal Father, Reshit – Beginning
Image: A face full on

Divine Aspect

Hebrew Divine Name: *Yah* or *Jah*
Deities in other traditions: Ptah – Egyptian Architect of the Universe, Pallas Athena – Greek Goddess of wisdom, Minerva – Roman Goddess of wisdom, Nuit – Egyptian Goddess of the starry night sky and Mother of Isis, Sophia – Gnostic Goddess of wisdom
Spiritual Paths: Father God worship – Judaism, Christianity, Islam

Correspondences in the Physical Universe

In the Cosmos: Mazlot – Zodiac or fixed stars, the cosmos
Colour: Grey
Number: 2

Correspondences in Humankind

Spiritual Experience: Vision of the Divine face-to-face
Positive quality: Devotion
In the human body: Brain and eyes

A WOMAN'S KABBALAH

Notes

1. Also translated as 'illuminating'.
2. From Moses Cordovero, *Tomer Devorah*, *Palm Tree of Deborah*. *Tomer Devorah* is an ethical treatise on the Imitation of God. First published in Venice in 1588.
3. Kaplan (1989, page 93).
4. Sigmund Freud (1927) *The Future of an Illusion*, Penguin Freud Library. London: Penguin Books.
5. Sigmund Freud (1910) 'Leonardo da Vinci and a Memory of His Childhood' in *The Standard Edition of the Complete Works of Sigmund Freud* (1953–74) (24 vols.). London: Hogarth Press and the Institute of Psychoanalysis.
6. Chana Ullman (1982) Cognitive and emotional antecedents of religious conversion, *Journal of Personality and Social Psychology*, 43, (pages 183–92).

3

BINAH – UNDERSTANDING OR INTELLIGENCE

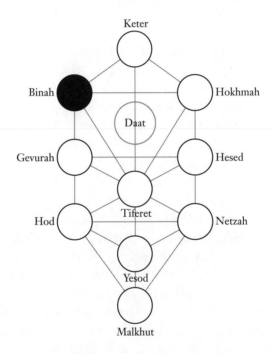

The third path is called 'Sanctifying Consciousness' (Sekhel MeKudash).
It is the foundation of Primordial Wisdom
and is termed 'Faithful Faith'.[1]
Its roots are AMeN.
It is the Mother of Faith,
and Faith originates from it.

SEFER YETZIRAH

Binah is Understanding, also translated as Intelligence. To understand we must develop the skill of listening. Keter is associated with thought and Binah with understanding that thought. The Divine in Keter thinks, 'I am'. This creates a movement within the Divine. That movement is Hokhmah. At Binah, the Divine becomes aware of Its thought as though it is an inner voice. The voice is perceived as something 'outside' or 'other'. This is Binah. The thought of Keter is heard by the 'ear' of Binah and pondered upon. Origin (Keter) and energy (Hokhmah) have created a Third dimension.

THE BEGINNING OF MATTER

With the Supernal Three, the Triad of Keter, Hokhmah and Binah, we have origin, becoming and end state. We have past, present and future. We have change, movement and time. We have the beginning of the Time–Space continuum. In Hokhmah, we have pure energy. It cannot contain anything and is like a flame that burns. At Binah the energy of Hokhmah is differentiated into different types of energy. Binah begins to order the chaos of Hokhmah. We begin to have the possibility of particles that can evolve into form or matter. In Kabbalah, matter (earth) is created by the interaction of the other three traditional elements – air or breath (Keter) with fire and water. Rabbi Aryeh Kaplan, a Kabbalistic scholar and the youngest physicist ever to be employed by the United States government[2] equated fire with electromagnetic force, water with the strong nuclear force that binds the atomic nucleus together, and air with the cohesive force that counters electromagnetic repulsion within the particle itself. These interactions allow light particles such as electrons to exist.

Energy travels not in straight lines but in curves. Light and other forms of energy must inevitably curve back on themselves. They return to their starting point changed by the journey and interact with their origin to create something new. We move from the realm of the oval in Hokhmah to that of interconnecting spirals in Binah. The spiral is frequently a Goddess symbol. Ancient Neolithic burial chambers in which the dead were returned to the Mother Goddess were frequently decorated with spirals. The image of the maze is also strongly associated with Goddess worship and is found still in the thirteenth-century cathedral of Chartres in France, built on a site dedicated originally to Celtic Goddess worship. Another spiral is found not in human-made structures but in biological structures – the spiral of DNA, the genetic coding material that gives rise to life.

THE DIVINE IN BINAH

In Kabbalah, the Divine is both female and male. Binah is associated with the female aspect of deity.

Bereshit bera Elohim et hashamaim vaat haaretz.
(In the beginning Elohim created Heaven and Earth.)

These are the first seven words of the Torah and the beginning of the Bible. In Judaism, the Torah is connected to Hokhmah, Wisdom. It is said to be the epitome of Hokhmah. Before reading the Torah, it is customary to say, 'Blessed art Thou, Holy One of the Universe, who has guided us to immerse ourselves in the words of the Torah.' The devout Jewish Kabbalist reads the Torah on many levels. These are conveyed by the word *pardes*, which means an orchard or pleasure garden. *Pardes* is symbolic of the spiritual state that the devout seeker attains in his or her studies of the mysteries. It is also an acronym based on its letters. These show that there are four levels of interpretation of sacred text, represented by the letters p, r, d and s. These are *p'shat* – the literal level, *remez* – the symbolic meaning of the literal text, *d'rash* – the inquiry between *p'shat* and *remez*, and *sod* – the hidden spiritual message that relates directly to the person reading the text. Whenever we read sacred texts (of whatever faith), we must strive for Binah, Understanding, by applying the techniques of *pardes*. We must ask ourselves – what do the words mean literally, what are they implying symbolically, what do we learn from the literal and symbolic meanings, and what hidden message is there here to help me in my everyday life at the present time?

The Hebrew Divine name used in the first seven words of the Torah is the Hebrew Divine Name in Binah – *Elohim*. Elohim comes from a root that means strength, might or power. The English translation often reads that a male 'God' created Heaven and Earth. This is incorrect. The word 'Elohim' is a plural noun. We could translate it as 'Gods' or 'Goddess and God', but Kabbalah makes it explicit that Elohim is female. In the *Zohar*, for instance, Elohim is called 'She' and Moses is described as 'husband of Elohim' to signify his mystical marriage with the feminine aspect of the Divine.[3]

In early times, people worshipped the Mother of All Living, the Great Goddess, as the supreme deity. A long drawn-out battle was fought for the hearts and minds of the people of Israel as the followers of Yahweh fought to establish their aspect of deity as supreme. If you read the Jewish Bible, the *Tanakh*[4] – an acronym for the Torah (the five books of Moses), Nevi'im (Prophets) and Ketuvim (Writings) – you will find constant references to Goddess worship. Hebrew women are described as ritually weeping at the annual festival to commemorate the death of Tammuz, son–consort of the Goddess Ishtar (Ezekiel 8:14). They bake cakes to honour the 'Queen of Heaven' (Jeremiah 7:17–18). They weave hangings to honour the Goddess Asherah (2 Kings 23:7). There is evidence that Goddess worship continued from 1000 BCE to 70 CE, from the time of the monarchy to the destruction of the Second Temple. The Goddess is cast out, but returns, cast out again and returns again. Christianity finally made an accommodation with the Goddess, by making the Virgin Mary a quasi-Goddess. In Kabbalah, the Divine Feminine retained her importance. The idea of the Goddess could not die.

It is natural for us to worship what is most mysterious and powerful. To our early ancestors the mystery of procreation, the ability to replicate ourselves, was the most wondrous of magics, so they worshipped it. In later times, as metal weapons were invented for warfare, men came to worship powerful male deities who might help them in battle. The worshippers of the Supernal Father supplanted those of the Supernal Mother.

If Hokhmah is associated with movement and Keter with the first thought, Binah is associated with the creation of light in the universe. In the Bible, Elohim is quoted as saying (Genesis 1:3), 'Let there be light', and there was light. Prior to this all was darkness. Once we have light, we have the potential for colour. The *Zohar* tells us that people in an ordinary state of consciousness cannot see the true colours of the higher sefirot. They can be seen by those in an exalted mystical state, but this is only achievable by those of great spiritual purity. The colours used in the Western Mystery Tradition to represent the Supernal Triad are white for Keter, grey for Hokhmah and black for Binah. Even if these colours are more symbolic than actual, they are useful concepts. Keter derives its whiteness from the light of Ain Sof Aur. We can imagine the light of Ain Sof Aur diminishing as it moves further away from its source. In Hokhmah that light decreases as it moves further away from the centre and begins to fade into greyness. In Binah, the original light is lost, but Binah starts the process of creating its own lights within the cosmos . . . the stars. The stars illuminate the darkness of the cosmos and life can begin. Binah is Mother to a cycle of creation. This cycle of creation will eventually atrophy and collapse in on itself, until the awareness of Keter and energy of Hokhmah surge forth once more and Binah creates again. Hail to the Creatrix of the Universe! Or as Tantric scripture says:

Obeisance be to Her who is pure Being-Consciousness-Bliss,
as Power who exists in the form of Time and Space
and all that is therein,
and who is the radiant Illuminatrix in all beings.[5]

The sefirot from Hokhmah to Gevurah are the source of archetypes. These are ideas that are pre-programmed in the human psyche. From the archetypes evolve our images of the Gods. The deities of different peoples, even though they go by different names, have a strong resemblance to one another. This is because all of humankind inherits a similar psyche. Whatever our colour or creed, our common human inheritance is stronger than anything that separates or differentiates us.

Psychologist Carl Jung believed that the human psyche was programmed so strongly to manifest particular archetypes that even if all the world's cultures were destroyed by some disaster, the archetypes would appear in our dreams and visions to help us recreate what had gone before. The archetypes are what we think of as 'Gods'. These powerful images come to us via the unconscious mind and seize hold of our imagination. They are found in all times and in all cultures. Due to cultural needs, particular archetypes dominate cultures at particular times. If important archetypes are repressed, for instance the female aspect of deity, then our unconscious need for them grows. Suddenly there is a popular upsurge in visions of these archetypes. Thus at various times the Jewish people have shown a strong need for the female aspect of Divinity – the Shekhinah. In the same way, Christians have turned to Virgin Mary and modern Hinduism is experiencing a strong revival of Kali worship. In many modern Western societies people have become increasingly interested in the Great Mother Goddess and in spiritual paths that venerate Her.

TIME AND FATE

Just as there are feminine aspects of Hokhmah in the form of wisdom personified as Sophia, so there are masculine aspects of Binah. Deities associated with Binah include the Greek Kronos or Father Time and the Roman Saturn, who is also associated with time and old age. Once we have the beginnings of matter, we have creation and destruction, new and old, building up and breaking down. In other words we have change. Time is a measurement of change. Once we have form, we have time and therefore ageing.

In the Norse tradition, Time is associated with three Goddesses, the Three Fates or Norns who represent Past, Present and Future and so have knowledge of all things. They continually weave the fabric of destiny and at the same time unravel it, an image that tells us that the present is continually being created and destroyed. In Hindu theology, creation is Maya, rather like a woven veil. It is illusion. What does this mean? If we think of the way that our senses process the inputs they receive from material creation, you will realize that it is truly illusion. What we perceive as solid is but atoms temporarily locked together in molecules that at the same time constantly move and change. In reality, nothing is solid or permanent. It is rather as though we are seeing reality through a very fast moving camera. When we see the world through a slowed-down camera, then we can see change. If you have watched television footage of flowers opening you will know what I mean.

TITLES AND IMAGES

Binah's ancient titles give clues about its nature. She is the Supernal Mother, *Imma Ila'ah*. The Western Mystery Tradition differentiates her into the bright and the dark and links these phases to the female life cycle. *Aima* is the Bright Fertile Mother and *Ama*, the Crone. The Crone is the stage when all is darkness. The Fertile Mother is the stage when Binah produces light. The idea that manifest creation proceeds from the Mother fits well with early notions of creation and fertility. In connection with Hokhmah, I mentioned early creation myths where the image of the Creatrix is that of a female bird laying a sacred egg that in time will hatch out the cosmos. The famous 16th-century Kabbalist Moses Cordovero interpreted a passage in Deuteronomy 22:6–7, which speaks of a mother bird seated in her nest with her young ones, as an image of Binah hatching out the lower sefirot.

In many spiritual traditions, we have the concept of a Creatrix Goddess who weaves the worlds, like Spider Woman of the Hopi. All weaver Goddesses express something of the nature of Binah. If we think of the beginning of creation, it is as though a great cosmic mind wove the particles, neutrons, electrons, atoms and molecules of the first matter into the complexity that is our universe today. This occurred slowly, patiently, over billions of years.

Binah is associated with the planet Saturn, a planet that moves much more slowly than our own Earth. Hokhmah bursts forth with the creative energy of fire – fire that can be quickly extinguished. Binah is associated with the element of water and sea.[6] This is not so much 'sea' as in oceans, but the cosmic sea. However, our Earthly sea gives us clues about Binah's nature. The sea has substance and shape, but that shape is not fixed. We have matter but we do not yet have fixed form.

The image of Binah is of a mature queen upon a throne. If you are familiar with the tarot, the image is not unlike those of the Queen of Pentacles or the Empress. We have here a sense of stability and of the ancient order of things. We have that which creates civilizations. One of Binah's titles is linked to this image. Binah is also known as *Khorsia*, the Throne. To our ancestors, the throne represented the government. It was a symbol of the stability of the state, rather as the White House, the Senate, Buckingham

Palace, or the Houses of Parliament would be to Americans or Britons today. In fact, the first letter of Binah is Bet, which is known as the house. This helps indicate the stabilizing influence of Binah. The association of the queen with the image of the throne is found in many cultures. In ancient Egyptian culture, the Goddess Isis was always depicted as seated on a throne and the Queen of Egypt was known as the throne. In Egypt, as in many ancient cultures, although the king ruled, he ruled by virtue of his marriage to a woman of royal blood. In other words inheritance was matrilinear. Only the son of a royal mother could inherit and he could only inherit if he married a woman of royal blood.

BINAH AND INDIVIDUAL DEVELOPMENT

In Hokhmah, we move outwards from the source of our being, Keter. In Binah, it is as though having been born, we turn round to behold our source and origin. We see our beginning point. We become aware of another who is separate from ourselves. Another image is that the cry of 'I am' projects us outwards into the universe. We turn and see our origin and realize that our origin and we are no longer one. We have been propelled out of the vagina. The umbilical cord that kept us attached to Keter has not yet been cut, but we become aware of our separation and isolation. We are still attached to the Mother, but we are no longer part of her. We are separate individuals. We receive and evaluate this information. We have the beginnings of Intelligence and Understanding. Binah is associated with the future in Kabbalah and Hokhmah with the past. There is only one past but there are many futures. At Binah we begin to have to choose. We have the beginning of free will.

BINAH QUALITIES

The virtue or positive quality of Binah is Silence. Its negative aspect is avarice or greed. What does this tell us? Silence means not reacting, maintaining one's own counsel. In order to understand we need to listen and to weigh what we have heard in the heart, the realm of intuitive feeling. We need to cultivate the silence of contemplation. There is a phrase in the Christian Bible which describes the Virgin Mary, having experienced all the strange happenings surrounding her son's birth, as 'treasuring all these things and reflecting on them in her heart'.[7] This is an image of Binah as Great Mother Goddess – listening, contemplating and weighing up what must be done. In ancient times, the heart was considered the organ of deep thought. We also talk of 'listening with the heart'. In modern Kabbalah, we might want to consider equating Binah with the ear, the organ of listening, as well as or instead of the heart.

At Binah, we must take in the Wisdom emanated by Hokhmah and digest it. We must work it over in our minds and come to an understanding of it. To understand, we must categorize and name. Binah represents that state of consciousness in which we meditate upon what we have experienced so far and learn to make use of it. What emerges into mind from this digestive process is the next stage of development of the Tree of Life, which is Daat or Knowledge. Knowledge is the fruit of the Tree of Life. When we eat of that fruit a new cycle begins.

Avarice or greed is the negative side of Binah. The purpose of understanding is not to gain knowledge for knowledge's sake, but to make use of that understanding. To make use of that understanding requires that we give out and communicate. The outward movement of Binah becomes the energy of Hesed, the sefirah that follows Binah. If we do not go forward, we atrophy and die. This is the problem of avarice. Avarice is a greed that is a kind of anal retention. We want to hold onto things, to keep them for ourselves and not to let go. This is poison and death.

SPIRITUAL EXPERIENCE OF BINAH

The spiritual experience of Binah is the Vision of Sorrow. Why should the beginning of matter and the third dimension cause sorrow? One component of the sorrow of Binah is the realization that inevitably incarnation means death. We become individual and attain the precious gift of consciousness. We become separate and we know loneliness. This is painful, but as we grow to adolescence and adulthood the pain passes and we forget. We come to love our sense of individuality and autonomy. As we approach the end of incarnation we realize the pain of incarnation in matter. We are in bodies that must inevitably fail us. To enjoy consciousness we must accept the inevitability of ageing and death, the separation from the body. There is also sorrow in a cosmic and less personal sense. The cosmos itself is not eternal. The Divine Oneness has created this extraordinary thing of beauty that is our universe, but in time the universe will collapse and die. All the wondrous creation of the Divine in Nature and all the conscious beings of the universe, with their art, literature and music, will one day be lost, never more to be seen. Form is not static. Form and structure cannot endure forever. They are continually worked upon by the energy of Hokhmah. At the level of Malkhut, matter appears to us to be stable, but this is an illusion. Matter is constantly decaying and changing. A static universe could not exist. It would be a dead universe. Instead we have the energy of Hokhmah being constantly formed and reformed by Binah in myriad new and more beautiful and wondrous ways. In time the impetus that is Keter, the thought process that creates our cosmos, must die away. Its impetus will lessen and our universe will begin to lose the power to regenerate and change itself. It will collapse in on itself and will be no more. This is the sorrow of Binah.

The bereavement that we suffer with the loss of those close to us is another aspect of the sorrow of Binah. One of the most terrible bereavements is that of a small child who loses her or his mother. Mother is the person who makes our small world safe. In our physical closeness to her we sense protection. When this is gone, we are alone and frightened. One of the most frightening children's films ever is *Bambi*, the eponymous story of a small deer who loses his Mother. Can you remember an experience of losing your mother, perhaps in the street or in a big department store? As small persons, we are unable to see far. The adult bodies that block our view restrict our vision. To lose our mothers in a crowd is terrifying indeed. How much more terrifying then for the child who loses her or his mother altogether. Other adults, grandparents, step-mothers and aunts, may try and replace the mother, but the biological bonding between mother and child is such that this is very difficult. If the relationship with our mothers is terminated prematurely, such as through death or desertion, we may be bound forever to an image of a mother who is both perfect, because she is seen with a child's uncritical eye, but abandoning. If our parents abandon us, we are inclined to think it must somehow be our fault. We are somehow unworthy. There can also be huge and unresolved problems of anger. The loss of a mother may impact on our adolescent and adult worlds by making it difficult to form relationship with others. We may feel that if we get too close we are bound to be abandoned or will get hurt. We may seek mother substitutes or may seek too quickly to become parents ourselves to blot out our loss.

If we have experienced the sorrow of bereavement, it is important to acknowledge it, but to hold on too long is a negative quality of Binah. The law of the universe is change and we have to let go and move forward. Grief is a necessary emotion but at some point we have to turn away from what is behind us and past towards what is future and potential. We turn from death to life.

An aspect of Binah's sorrow is the pain of separation. For the first two years of life, the infant is closely bonded with the mother. In earlier cultures the infant might have been bound to the mother's back. Usually children were held by the mother or, when she was unavailable, by another relative. Infants were not placed in rooms on their own. In today's culture we may experience aloneness at an earlier stage, but the psychic bond with the mother in the first two years is very strong. Mothers are often instinctively aware of any danger to their child and the faintest cry will arouse a mother from the deepest sleep. At the age of two, we start to become our own person and if we have good parenting, our parents will encourage this. If we have parents who hold on too long to the bond, we may find it difficult to assert our own individuality and to break free. Separation is difficult, but acquiring autonomy is an important part of Binah.

Binah is often described as the womb of the universe, but it is better thought of as the vagina. Keter is the womb in which all creation is gestated and made ready for birth. In Keter is the quickening, the stirring to life. At Hokhmah it is as though we are expelled down the birth canal. A movement begins which is unstoppable, but we are not yet separate from our origin. At Binah we are thrust into the world. We enter the world with a cry of rage, fear and outrage at this terrible thing that is happening to us. We are separated from the source of our being at Keter. The umbilical cord is cut and we become our own person. In the Tree of Life, there is a void between the Supernal Triad of Keter, Hokhmah and Binah, and the sefirot that follow. This is known as the Abyss. With the cutting of the umbilical cord, we are thrust away from the source of our being across to the far side of the Abyss. We enter the world by one route. We will have to find another way to return. We cannot re-enter the womb: there is no path back from Hesed to Binah, the next sefirah on the Tree.

EXPLORING BINAH

EXERCISE 1: THE GREAT MOTHER GODDESS

This is an exercise to help to sense what it might mean to see the Divine as feminine and what role the Divine Mother might play in your life. The exercise takes up to an hour. You will need to be alone in a quiet room. If it is daytime, shut out any bright light. At night have only soft unobtrusive lighting or candlelight. You will need some plain paper, a pen to write, and some paints or coloured pens or pencils. You could write or type out the exercise in large print so that you can see it by dim lighting. Alternatively you could read it onto a cassette so you can play it back to yourself. If you read the exercise onto a cassette, leave gaps for visualization between each instruction.

1. Close your eyes and take a few moments to relax. Then begin to visualize.
2. It is a starlit night. There is no moon, but the stars are very bright and there is sufficient light to see. You are walking on a sandy shore by the edge of an ocean. There is no wind, so the sea is still with scarcely a wave. All is silent.
3. You look away from the sea towards the land behind. On the horizon you can make out a dark outline against the sky. You see there is a path leading from the shore to the silhouette against the sky. You fol-low the path.
4. You find that you are approaching a raised marble dais on which is a throne of dark brown wood. Three tall black marble pillars surround

the dais, reaching up to the starry sky above. As you gaze at the throne you see that the sky is getting a little lighter. You turn around to look at the sea. Grey and pink streaks are appearing in the sky as though dawn might be approaching.

5. You sense a great peace and holiness in this place, as though you are at the dawn of time. You kneel in front of the dais. As you do so, you sense that you are no longer alone.

6. When you look up, you see that a woman is seated upon the throne. She is veiled so that you cannot see her face, but you sense a presence of great power and mystery. She is the first feminine principle and the source of all womanhood. She says nothing, but it is as though she is communicating with you directly by thought.

7. You hear her asking:
   - What do you seek?
   - How can I help you?
   - How can I heal you?
     Take five minutes to talk with her to find out how she can help or heal you.

8. You may wish to ask yourself some questions:
   - What are your feelings about the Divine Feminine in your own life?
   - What part can she play?
     Take some time for this.

9. When you have finished, bid farewell to the Goddess. It is time to leave this place. Go back to the sea, along the path by which you came. Sit down by the edge of the waves. You hear the sound of the waves lulling you to sleep.

10. You rest for a while and then wake refreshed. You are back in your own room, your own dwelling place.

11. Make notes on your experiences. Write down any thoughts that come to you. Perhaps draw or paint what you have seen. Here are some questions to help you:
    - What was the pathway like that took you to the Goddess?
    - Was it easy or hard?
    - Although she was veiled, what impression did you have of the woman behind the veil? Was she old or young, beauty or crone, or maybe all or none of these?

- What do you seek from the Goddess?
- How can she heal you?
- How can she help you?
- What part can she play in your life?

EXERCISE 2: THE TEMPLE OF SILENCE

Silence is something those of us who live in urban settings rarely experience. Even at night, in the background is the faint throb of overhead aircraft, the distant roar of traffic, the wail of police sirens, the rattle of trains, and voices of passers-by in the street. In Nature too there is rarely silence. We have bird song by day, or by night the hoots of owls, the rustling of leaves in the wind, the scuffling noises of those creatures that hunt by night. When Nature is silent, it is usually a sign of impending danger. Birds cease to sing just before a tornado, earthquake, hurricane, or total eclipse of the sun.

Silence can be a beautiful sound. Have you ever heard the ringing silence that is found in a temple, church or other holy place? This silence has a special quality. It is both non-sound and a special sound of its own. It is as though we can almost touch the air, the atmosphere seems so latent with something holy and special. It refreshes us to experience silence. Silence takes us back to the origin of things. This is an exercise to help you experience a place of silence.

1. Close your eyes and take a few moments to relax. Then begin to visualize.
2. It is a starlit night. There is no moon but the stars are very bright and there is sufficient light to see. You are walking on a sandy shore by the edge of the ocean. The waves lap the shore and you smell salt upon the air. Apart from the soft lulling sound of the sea, all is silent.
3. You look away from the sea towards the land behind. On the horizon you can make out a dark shape. You see there is a path leading from the shore to the silhouette against the sky. You follow the path.
4. You find that you are approaching a raised marble dais on which is a throne of dark brown wood. Three tall black marble pillars surround the dais, reaching up to the starry sky above.

5. You sit or kneel by the throne and rest your hands upon its wooden smoothness. You say softly or in your mind a chant.

Temple of Silence Chant[8]
In the Temple of Silence,
I shall adore you.
I shall cherish you.

In the Temple of Silence,
I shall cherish you,
I shall love you.

In the Temple of Silence,
I shall love you,
I shall worship you.

In the Temple of Silence,
I shall worship you,
I shall adore you.

Then say:

Prayer of Praise to the Goddess
Blessed Be the Great Mother,
without beginning and without ending,
Blessed Be her temple of pure black marble,
Blessed Be the stillness of her holy place.
Blessed Be the wave that caresses the shore for her,
Blessed Be the sand that succumbs to its embrace,
Blessed Be the shell that is cast up from her,
Blessed Be She, the Mother of Pearl.
Blessed Be She,
Blessed Be.[9]

You can use this chant whenever you need inner peace.

6. Sit for a while and enjoy the feeling of peace, then when you are ready, return by the way you came.

EXERCISE 3: UNDERSTANDING THE FEMININE

Binah is the Mother archetype, that most powerful figure of the world of our infancy. For both women and men, our mothers teach us both consciously and unconsciously what it means to be a woman. Here are some questions for you to think about to see how your mother may have influenced your views about women. Find a time when you can be alone for an hour to think about your answers. You might like to write down or type up the questions and your answers so that you can keep them.

1.   What is your earliest memory of your mother? Try to visualize her.
   • What is she wearing?
   • Does she seem happy or sad, relaxed or exhausted, peaceful or worried and agitated?
   • Was she confident or anxious? If anxious, what frightened her? Was it the world, financial difficulties, material instability, your father?

2.   What was her relationship with your father like?
   • Was it loving and companionable?
   • Was it argumentative?
   • Had he abandoned her or she him?
   • What early impressions did your mother's relationship with your father give you of male–female relationships?

3.   Did your mother value other women?
   • Did she have women friends and were they supportive of one another?
   • Did your mother prefer friendships with men or with women?
   • Did she respect or look down on other women?
   • Did she see other women as rivals, preferring to be the adored of men, or was she comfortable in mixed company?

- Did she put women down and denigrate their abilities, or did she praise them?
- Was she scornful or jealous of successful women, or did she admire their achievements?
- Was she a successful woman herself?
- What messages did she leave you about the worth of women?
- If you are a woman: did she favour your brothers or other male relatives over you, or vice versa?

4. Was she satisfied with the men in her life, or were they never 'good enough' and always at fault?
    - If you are a man: what messages did you absorb about yourself as a man?

These are just a few questions to help you think about the messages that your mother may have conveyed to you consciously or unconsciously about the importance of women. Once you have answered them, think about your own relationships with women. Do you carry any negative images of women into those relationships? If so, think about what you can begin to change. If you feel that you have been programmed with negative messages about women, remember that Binah, while she may appear static, is constantly changing. Everything in our lives can change.

ONWARDS TO DAAT

We are propelled from the world of the Mother to Hesed, where the magical image is of a King upon a Throne. We are propelled from the world of the womb and nursery to the outer world of patriarchy; a world still dominated by men. We enter Hesed via Daat, the experience of Knowledge. Let us now turn to Daat.

Binah – Understanding, Intelligence

Titles: Imma Ila'ah – Supernal Mother, Khorsia – Throne, Teshuvah – Return, Aima – Bright fertile Mother, Ama – Dark sterile Mother, the Palace
Images: Great Mother Goddess, a mature queen on a throne, a vast sea

Divine Aspect

Hebrew Divine Name: *Elohim* – Goddess and God, or simply Goddess
Deities in other traditions: Kronos – Greek Father Time and Saturn – Roman equivalent, Spider Woman – Hopi, Arachne – Greek spider Goddess, the three Norns or Fates – Norse Goddesses, Virgin Mary in Catholicism (not strictly a Goddess but treated as such)
Spiritual Paths: Goddess worship, some aspects of Kabbalah, Hinduism, Wicca, some Tibetan Buddhism, popular Catholicism

Correspondences in the Physical Universe

In the Cosmos: Shabbatai (Saturn)
Colour: Black
Number: 3

Correspondences in Humankind

Spiritual Experience: Vision of Sorrow
Positive quality: Silence
Negative quality: Avarice
In the human body: Ears and heart

Notes

1. Isaiah 25:1.
2. Kaplan (1997 ed., page 145).
3. Matt (1983, page 105).
4. Also written *Tenach*.
5. Avalon (1975 ed., page 27).
6. Some, such as Rabbi Aryeh Kaplan, equate Binah with Fire and Hokhmah with Water. I use here the Western Mystery Tradition attributions, but it is important to remember that all correspondences are merely symbols to help us explain reality. They are not reality itself.
7. Luke 2:19.
8. I am grateful to Maxine Sanders for teaching me the original version of this chant.
9. Based on Vivianne Crowley (1988) 'Prayer of Praise to the Goddess'.

DAAT - KNOWLEDGE

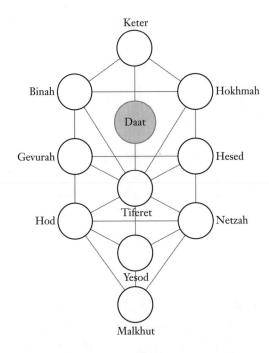

Keter

Binah

Hokhmah

Daat

Gevurah

Hesed

Tiferet

Hod

Netzah

Yesod

Malkhut

From my early childhood,
before my bones, nerves and veins were fully strengthened,
I have always seen this vision in my soul,
even to the present time, when I am more than seventy years old –
The light that I see thus is not spatial,
but it is far brighter than a cloud that carries the sun –
and I call it 'the reflection of the Living Light' –
and I see, hear, and know[1] all at once,
and as if in an instant, I know what I know.

ABBESS HILDEGARD VON BINGEN[2]

Between the sefirot of Binah and Hesed is an aspect of the Divine that is not a sefirah or emanation, but a state of consciousness that is the result of the interaction between Binah and Hokhmah. This is Daat, Knowledge. Daat, Knowledge, helps us approach closer to the Divine. No mention of Daat is found in the earliest kabbalistic texts, but references to Daat start to appear from the 13th century onwards. It is Daat consciousness that enables us in physical incarnation, with our limited physical brains and sensory organs, to have knowledge of that which is beyond sensory experience. The words of 12th-century German mystic Hildegard von Bingen quoted above try to convey the idea of inner 'knowing'. If we acquire Wisdom and Understand it, then we obtain Knowledge or Daat. Daat is considered an external reflection of Keter, which is beyond our understanding. In some ways Keter is like the Moon to the Sun of Ain Sof, Daat is Moon to Keter's Sun, and in the lower sefirot, Yesod is Moon to Tiferet's Sun. Daat is a state of advanced intuition. We sometimes access a more Yesodic version of this in our everyday lives when we have hunches and 'feelings'. We do not know how we know something, but we know it. We feel it in our bones. It is part of our consciousness. We just *know*. The highest level of 'knowing' to which we can aspire is Daat. At this level of consciousness, we have deep inner connection with the Divine.

THE DIVINE IN DAAT

Daat's Hebrew Divine name is first mentioned by Isaac Luria, leading Kabbalist of the 16th-century school in Safed, Palestine. By a complex process of Gematria (manipulating the numbers associated with each Hebrew letter), he combines names from Keter, Hokhmah and Binah to produce YAHHWHYHH. This name represents the 'Supernal Copulation' and the reuniting of Hokhmah and Binah. In the *Zohar*, we are told that the Divine Father is ever in union with or 'knows' the Divine Mother. Daat represents the male and female aspects of Divinity reunited once more after their separation into two at Hokhmah and Binah, but with the knowledge of their separate attributes retained. If Keter is neuter, then Daat is male and female with the potential and potencies of both force and form. The *Zohar* tells us that the Divine says of Itself, 'Any image that does not embrace male and female is not a high and true image.' The Divine is Goddess and God.

Daat translates as knowledge, but the knowledge that Daat imparts is not intellectual knowledge of theoretical Kabbalah, but an inner 'knowing' that is derived from meditative experience. This is a kind of unconscious knowledge. We are not consciously aware of it, but it influences our actions. If you want to think about how this might operate in the Divine realm, imagine that the Divine becomes conscious in Keter. Of course, the Divine is omnipotent – all-knowing and all-powerful. The Divine could choose to know the outcome of the creative process that It begins, but perhaps It chooses not to. Daat can be equated to unconscious knowledge that the Divine chooses not to consciously know.

KABBALAH AND MYSTICISM

Kabbalah can be divided into different branches in much the same way as Yoga. Commonly used is a threefold division: theoretical, meditative and magical. Theoretical Kabbalah is concerned with the theology and philosophy of Kabbalah. It is based on the *Zohar* and is concerned with learning about the spiritual domain. Meditative Kabbalah is the mystical tradition of Kabbalah approached through intuition and concerned with union with the Divine. Divine names and letter permutations are intoned to help the practitioner reach higher states of consciousness. These states lead to mystical realization, which may bring the ability to use magical powers – magical Kabbalah.

What is mysticism? There has always been a division in spiritual traditions between *exoteric* or outer religion, which is concerned with maintaining morality and social order, and *esoteric* religion, which has as its goal spiritual transformation. Mysticism goes beyond the external focus of religious practice, morality and dogma. It aspires to direct experience of the Divine. Meditative Kabbalah causes spiritual changes, which access certain magical powers. In Yoga, these powers are known as *siddhis*. Powers may be attained, but the attainment of these powers is not the aim of a dedicated Kabbalist. They are merely a side effect on the way to the ultimate aim of realization of the Divine.

TITLE AND IMAGES

Keter is often associated with Truth in Kabbalah, whereas Daat is *Shalom*, Peace. The word comes from the root *shalem*, perfect or complete. In the *Bahir*, Knowledge is described as that with which we recognize Truth.[3] In other words, Daat is that by which we recognize Keter. This is important because humankind cannot experience Keter directly and return intact. Keter is 'that which is attained at the End of Desire', the blue-white fire that consumes. If we encounter Keter we are absorbed back into the Divine Oneness and do not return. This is the story of Galahad and the Grail, or of the Grail Maiden, themes that are the foundation of Charles Williams' beautiful but now old-fashioned 1930s novels *War in Heaven* and *Many Dimensions*.

Knowledge implies memory. Daat is the repository of the memory of the universe, the 'Library at the end of the Universe'. Imagine a vast data bank of all that has happened to the cosmos in this cycle of its existence and you would be approaching the idea of Daat. Another image associated with Daat is the collective unconscious. There is an esoteric saying that, 'If that which thou seekest thou findest not within thee, thou wilt never find it without thee.' This means that there is a secret way to knowledge. Instead of enquiring outwards we enquire inwards. We meditate upon symbols and words and meaning comes from deep within us. We need to enter a deep meditative state in order to achieve this. Techniques to help people do this have been taught at the advanced level of all spiritual traditions. The *Sefer Yetzirah* is such a text.

Those who have studied mystical experience agree that it is both *noetic*, that it imparts Gnosis or knowledge, and that it is ineffable, or beyond words. Mystical experience is transitory. Daat is a sefirah in which we can glimpse briefly something of Keter before returning to our everyday state of consciousness. We return with the precious knowledge of the true nature of things. Those who have made this journey may become mystics, gurus or spiritual teachers. However, the original insight will often be distorted from the original experience. The personality of the mystic and his or her desires intrude and colour the experience to fit previous preconceptions and personal aims. This is inevitable; for the message of Daat is that there is no perfection this side of manifestation. Only in Unity (Keter) do we find perfection.

There are some images of Daat that have evolved in the Western Mystery Tradition. These include a void, a black hole, an empty room, a silver mirror, and a room with an empty throne, all of which convey the sense of absence and of not seeing what we expect to see. To enter Daat consciousness is to make the frightening discovery that our previous certainties about the nature of the Divine and the nature of the cosmos are flawed. Our experience is mediated by the sensory and processing limits of the human brain. We can perceive and process only a part of the true reality of existence. We form symbols and analogies to explain cosmic mysteries, but these are only that – symbols and analogies. Our knowledge of reality is on the level of a rather primitive computer simulation. At some point in our return journey to the Divine, we must trade in these toys for the real thing.

DAAT AND INDIVIDUAL DEVELOPMENT

In the human life cycle, Binah equates to our infancy when we are in close union with our mothers. It is the world of the nursery. We have not yet learned to make choices ourselves. We have not begun to exercise our free will and to make choices between good and evil. As we evolve from Binah we acquire free will. Daat represents leaving the world of the nursery and beginning to make our own decisions. We begin to explore who and what we are. The transition comes when we learn to speak. Daat can be associated in the body with the throat. We learn to give voice to our thoughts. We learn the names of the objects around us. We develop the power to communicate. We begin to ask questions and to store information. As we explore the world, we develop a fund of past experience to draw on. Another important development comes when we learn our own names. We begin to develop a concept of 'I'.

Daat is a sefirah that joins male and female. As we learn more about 'I', we acquire gender awareness. We realize that we are male or female. We begin to explore what this means. We seek what is often forbidden – knowledge of the body of the opposite sex. We begin to play games like 'hospitals' where we can find out more and question which bit of girls' anatomy babies emerge from. Curiosity is the driving force, and the quest for knowledge, even as they were for Eve in the Garden of Eden.

Kabbalah teaches that the first human beings were androgynous. The *Zohar* tells us that 'male–female, the Divine One created them and they were called Adam.' The *Zohar* teaches that Adam was the child of the Divine Mother and Father. Since female and male created Adam, Adam was 'in the image of the Divine, male and female' (Genesis 1:27). When Hokhmah and Binah unite at Daat, they produce the first of humankind, a divine spark in a human body. Usually the Hebrew word *tzela* is translated as 'rib'; suggesting that Eve, who is known as Mother of All, was made from Adam's rib. However *tzela* is more properly translated as 'side'. The original human being, Adam, was divided into two – a male side who retained the name Adam and a female side, Eve.

Most people will be familiar with the Genesis story in the Bible where Eve persuades Adam to taste of the fruit of the only tree that has been forbidden them. This is the central tree of the Garden of Eden, the Tree of Knowledge of Good and Evil. As any parent will know, the surest way to get a young being to do something is to tell him or her not to do it. Since we can suppose that the Divine is not stupid, this prohibition has an inevitable and pre-planned outcome. A serpent slithers up to Eve and whispers an intriguing proposal: if Eve and Adam eat of the fruit of Knowledge of Good and Evil, they will become 'as Gods'. Of course, the serpent does not promise that it will be pleasurable for an incarnate being to possess Divine insight.

In the story of the Garden of Eden, eating the fruit of the Tree of Knowledge brings about a consciousness shift whereby our early human ancestors awaken to self-awareness and are thrust out of the Garden of Eden. The myth can be read on many levels. We awaken from our animal state and realize our own mortality, the nature of human consciousness and our need for unity with the Divine. It can also be read that the apples give us knowledge of our sexual difference and a sense in Eve and Adam of their separateness. Instead of being twin souls, they become individual and become embarrassed by the sexual difference between them, at the same time as they are attracted by it.

Gender awareness hits Eve and Adam when they eat of the Tree of Knowledge. Sexuality begins to involve individual interaction rather than simple biological urges. Gender is considered fundamental in our society; so much so that parents traditionally dressed baby boys and baby girls in different colour clothes in case anyone made a mistake. It is only after we have absorbed our gender identity that formal education begins.

At Daat in individual development, we begin to gain independence. We begin to understand good and evil, right and wrong. We become able consciously to do things we know to be bad. In Daat, our actions are no longer pure and unsullied. We acquire guilt and shame. In the Biblical story of the Garden of Eden, once Adam and Eve have eaten of the Tree of Knowledge, they know shame. They cover themselves with leaves. They feel they have something to hide. At Daat, we become capable of embarrassment and shame, when our behaviour does not meet the standards we are taught. Even if we are not 'caught' we may know shame or guilt. All this is the product of the eating of the fruit of the Tree of Knowledge that awakens us from our unknowing animal state, but at the same time awakens within us a sense of duality. We become that which looks and that which looks upon. We become mirror and viewer, image and gazer upon that image. We lose our inner sense of unity with our environment and with those around us.

HUMAN QUALITIES AND DAAT

The Virtue of Daat is often given by modern Western Mystery Tradition Kabbalists as detachment. Daat involves preparing to detach from the parental home and to go forth into the world. Although we may be physically detached, many people are not psychologically detached from their parents, in the sense of being able to take an objective view of the relationship. Much of growing up is about disillusionment when we realize that our parents are not perfect beings and that they have faults. Some people never get over this stage. They spend years in psychotherapy bewailing the fact that their mother and father did not bring them up in the right way, or were not good enough parents. The truth is of course that people are the product of their environment and those whose parenting skills are poor are usually themselves the offspring of bad parenting. Cycles and patterns of poor parenting or even abuse are perpetuated down the generations, until someone has the saving knowledge, Gnosis, and says, 'Stop. Let us change.'

EXPLORING DAAT

EXERCISE 1: DRAWING THE TREE OF LIFE

You are beginning to form a picture in your mind of the relationship between the different sefirot. It will help you if you draw and colour an image of the sefirot as they link to one another on the path of manifestation. The diagram that you will see at the front of each chapter of this book shows the Tree of Life with a complex set of paths, some of which relate to manifestation and some to the re-absorption of the manifest world into the Divine – and many permutations in between.

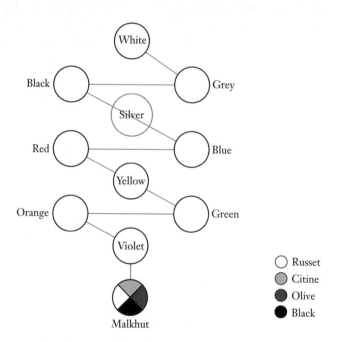

The Lightning Flash (Path of Manifestation) with Sefirot Colours

Here is another, simpler diagram called the 'Lightning Flash'. Traditionally it was thought that once manifestation began, the process was completed within seven days. We now know that these 'days' represent millions of years. Of course, these are long periods in comparison with the human life span, but they are little more than blinks of the eye to the Divine.

Take some white card and coloured pens, pencils or paints and make your own diagram of the lightning flash. You could trace this one or draw your own. It is important to colour the sefirot, as the colour will stimulate your imagination. Leave the diagram propped up somewhere you can see it every day, such as on your desk, pinned to the refrigerator or a kitchen cupboard, or by the bathroom mirror. This will help fix the relationship between the different sefirot in your mind.

EXERCISE 2: A CANDLE BLESSING

One of the attributes of Daat is peace. Many meditative exercises can help you feel more peaceful. The Prayer of Praise at the end of Chapter One on Keter will help you feel centred and ready to face the world. The Candle Blessing is another simple exercise that you could perform at home. To our ancestors, the igniting of flame was a miraculous act. Control over the element of fire helped our evolution from our animal to human state and there is still something magical to our psyches about flame and fire. You could perform this blessing every day, but that might be rather ambitious if you have a lot of other preoccupations in your life. Try setting aside one evening each week to do the Candle Blessing, preferably on the same day each week. You will need about half an hour for the exercise.

1. Find a small table, shelf or window that you can clean and tidy. You could put a vase of flowers on it, and you could cover it with a cloth if you wish.
2. Place two candlesticks with candles on the surface. The candles can be any colour you wish. You will need matches or a lighter to light the candles.
3. Dim all other lights in the room and place a chair so that you can to sit in front of your candles. You could sit on the floor if this is easier.
4. Now light your candles and as you light them begin to say the words below.

With the lighting of this flame,
let blessings extend from the Divine to all humankind;
let the light of Knowledge be sought and found.
Blessed be the Divine throughout the heavens,
Blessed be the Divine beyond the worlds,
Blessed be the Divine ascending,
Blessed be the Divine descending,
Blessed be the Divine in matter,
Blessed be the Divine in space,
Blessed be the Divine within the heart of all.
Blessed be.

5.   Now sit peacefully for a while and allow all the tensions of the day to fade. Imagine above your head the Divine light of Keter. The light flows over you, bathing your body in its cleansing luminance, washing away all tensions, cares, tiredness and anxiety. It flows into you – through your pores, filling your skull, your neck, your trunk, your legs, arms and even down to your hands and feet – filling you with its essence.

6.   When you feel rested and at peace in the light of the Divine, ask for any assistance you need in your daily life. Ask for the insight and the knowledge that you need to make decisions that are wise and worthy of the person you are and the person you would like to become.

7.   Then when you have finished, prepare to extinguish the candles. For a short period you have made your home a temple, by inviting the light of the Divine Being into it. Once you have extinguished your candles, say the words below to acknowledge the Presence of the Divine that you have invoked into your life.

The flame is extinguished for a time,
leaving behind a place of Peace.
Let not our steps falter, nor our courage fail,
though the journey is long and the dangers many.
Let us know the deep and transforming love,
that triumphs over despair,
the giver of hope,

until we see at last the Golden Dawn,
the rise of the light accomplished,
and the Knowledge of the Presence made known to all.
Let blessings extend to the Divine from all humankind.
Let tomorrow's flame burn ever more brightly,
as we walk along the way of eternal evolution into Deity.
The Shekhinah has withdrawn herself.
The Temple is closed.
Blessed be.

TO HESED

We have knowledge and once we have knowledge we can move forward. With knowledge of Its own being, the Divine can enter a new phase of evolution. Hokhmah gave us one urge to expansion. Hesed, the sefirah below Hokhmah, will give us the next.

Daat – Knowledge

Titles: Invisible Sefirah, Peace
Images: Void, black hole, an empty room, an empty throne, a silver mirror

Divine Aspect

Hebrew Divine Name: *YAHHWHYHH*
Spiritual Paths: Gnosticism, initiatory mystery traditions, mysticism in all traditions

Correspondences in the Physical Universe

In the Cosmos: Dark matter
Colour: Silver or ultra-violet
Number: none

Correspondences in Humankind

Positive quality: Detachment
Negative quality: Doubt
In the human body: Throat

Notes

1. See (Hokhmah), hear (Binah) and know (Daat).
2. Letter to Guibert of Gembloux (1175CE). Quoted in Barbara Newman (ed.) 1987.
3. Kaplan (1989, page 73).

HESED – MERCY

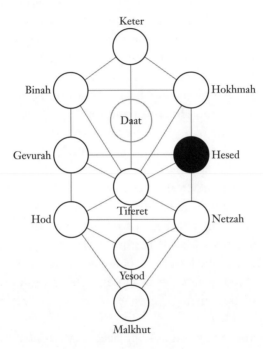

Keter

Binah

Hokhmah

Daat

Gevurah

Hesed

Tiferet

Hod

Netzah

Yesod

Malkhut

The fourth path is called 'Settled Consciousness' (Sekhel Kavua),
because all the spiritual powers emanate from it
as ethereal emanations.
Each emanates from the next by the power of Keter,
the primordial emanation.

SEFER YETZIRAH

Origin, movement, light, knowledge – we have Keter, Hokhmah, Binah and Daat – the awakening of awareness, energy, the beginning of form and the knowledge of what these things are. Without this conscious awareness of Its own nature, the Divine could not create. The Divine at Daat acquires knowledge of Its potential and stores this in memory. The Divine now has knowledge based on past experience. The Divine reaches out once more into the universe as it did with the second emanation of Hokhmah. It seeks to manifest all the myriad and multiple aspects of Itself that it can conceive. Hesed is therefore said to receive the outpouring of the Supernal Triad above it. Keter, Hokhmah and Binah represent states of being and energies that are far beyond human experience. We can develop ideas and analogies of these sefirot by thinking of how we have experienced the energies of 'Mother' and 'Father', for instance, in our own lives, but we are thinking of images and metaphors only and not of the ultimate reality of the Supernal Triad. Keter, Hokhmah and Binah are rather like a board of non-executive directors of a major corporation. They give a legal framework to the organization and advise and guide policy, but they are not involved in the day-to-day affairs of the corporation. They step in only if something goes badly wrong. It is the aspects of the Divine from Hesed onwards that are most involved in the cosmos as we know it.

Kabbalists call the first three sefirot *Mohin* or Mentalities. The next seven are *Midot* or Attributes. Mentalities are internal processes. Attributes are external qualities. The lower sefirot are qualitatively different from the Supernal Triad. At Hesed, we grow closer to our own human experience and the aspects of the Divine that we encounter from Hesed downwards are easier for us to relate to.

In Binah, Elohim creates light – the necessary essential for life. Light is an energy that partakes of the elemental qualities of both Air and Fire. Once we have sunlight we have the potential for biological life. In Hesed we see the next stage of creation emerge. These are unicellular organisms, single cells that are alive.

We often get the impression when we learn about our planet, that life has existed on it only recently. However, fossil evidence shows that it was relatively soon in our planet's life span – about 3,850 million years ago, less than 700 million years after the Earth's formation – that life emerged as simple single-celled organisms. Some of these organisms still exist, such as

Archaea, bacteria of ancient origin that today often live in hostile environments like hot springs. Many organisms emerged but only some survived the test of time. At Hesed the Divine mind conceives all that It can conceive. Nothing is censored. The Divine seeks to experience Itself without limitation. Here everything is possible. The Divine is brainstorming and manifesting every creative idea It can think of. Not all of these ideas will work. To sift and select the most viable ideas is the process of the next sefirah, Gevurah.

THE DIVINE IN HESED

Hesed is Mercy, an attribute of the Divine that receives strong emphasis in Judaism. This is celebrated in the 16th-century Kabbalistic text *Tomer Devorah* or *The Palm Tree of Deborah* by Rabbi Moses ben Jacob Cordovero.

> *Who is a Divinity like unto Thee, who bearest iniquity*
> *and passes by the transgression of the remnant of Thy heritage?*
> *Thou retainest not Thy anger forever,*
> *because Thou delightest in Mercy.*
> *Thou wilt again have compassion upon us;*
> *Thou wilt subdue our iniquities:*
> *and Thou wilt cast all their sins into the depths of the sea.*
> *Tomer Devorah*[1]

The Divine as Hesed is pure and absolute love. This is represented in the Bible by the Divine name *El*, meaning 'Mighty One' but often translated as 'God'. Here love does not mean love of another, but an outpouring of grace that seeks to possess nothing. The Divine awakens and pours forth Its own essence. What is love but an outward movement, a willingness to embrace the universe and all that it contains? Love at Hesed is unconditional love, the love that the Divine has for its creation. There is no reservation or hesitation in absolute love. It is a movement forward that absorbs wholly and without reservation all that it finds. Relationship implies a movement – love's movement is one of approach. Avoidance is about rejection and hate. Hesed's impulse is not judgemental movement, nor a movement of criticism or punishment, but a reaching out to someone or something that is different from Itself. It is like the love of parents of all species for their young offspring.

Divine Love is one of the most important and potent forces in the universe. The psychologist Carl Jung was talking about Hesedic love when he said that we are 'the victims of and the instruments of cosmogonic "love".'[2] By this, he did not mean the type of love that is about desire or wanting or need, but an outpouring of altruistic feeling that can inspire us to contribute to our communities. When we experience the Divine in Hesed, we experience a being who loves us perfectly and without reservation. Moses Cordovero in the *Palm Tree of Deborah* teaches that Hesed is Absolute Love.

TITLES AND IMAGES

The image of Hesed is of a mighty monarch on a throne. This is linked to Majesty, one of the titles of Hesed. Traditionally, the Divine images and names associated with Hesed have been predominantly male. In the Western Mystery Tradition, Hesed is associated with beneficent ruler Gods such as the Roman Jupiter and the Greek Zeus. These are deities who rule over prosperity and periods of economic expansion. The work of Hesed is to build, create and grow. Other images are of male parental care. In the Bible, the relationship between the Divine and humankind is often likened to that of shepherd and sheep. The shepherd's job has many activities that are often seen as the province of women. The shepherd acts as midwife to his sheep, helping them to give birth, often in the cold of deepest winter. He must rescue the sheep that are lost or injured. He must find new mothers for lambs whose own mothers have died and he must guard his sheep against predators such as wolves.

DEITIES AND SAINTS

In the Western Mystery Tradition, Hesed is the realm of deified human beings. Other than in brief mystical experiences, Hesed is the highest level of consciousness that humankind can achieve. Those advanced spirits who have reached Hesedic consciousness in incarnation are likely to be perceived as great spiritual teachers or saints. Some of the early Kabbalistic teachers fall into this category; people so removed from worldly concerns that they entered a state of eternal contemplation of the Divine. This is the realm of people such as Rabbi Moses Cordovero, one of the most renowned and prolific Kabbalists of the 16th century who was a profound exponent of the teachings of the *Zohar* and a leading figure in the circle of Kabbalist mystics who lived in 16th-century Safed in Palestine.

Some who transcend this state of consciousness and have transitory experiences of Daat where they behold the Divine may be deified as Gods. Buddha and Jesus are both worshipped by many of their followers as personal deities; even if this was not their intention. Mohammed's emphasis in Islam on not making images of deities, or indeed permitting any images of human beings in art, ensured that this was not his fate. The Prophet is revered as the equivalent of a great saint, but he is not seen as Divine.

Hesed is not only the realm of deified human beings, but also those who are considered great saints, teachers and gurus. These are people whose lives inspire us to live for an ideal. These are not mystics, but practical people who seek to impact upon the world rather than to withdraw from it. In Hinduism, we have the Indian leader Mahatma Gandhi whose methods of passive resistance destroyed colonial rule in British India. In Catholicism, we have figures such as Mother Theresa and, in Protestant tradition, Black leader Martin Luther King whose famous speech, 'I have a dream' spoke of unity between those of different races and creeds. They include those who strive to better society through peaceful means, and sometimes through peaceful protest. They have a moral strength that belies any physical weakness or lack of physical resources. They are those who change society through an unstoppable love. Leaders with the energy of Gevurah, the sefirah that follows Hesed, are often heads of armies and organizations. Hesedic leaders often begin outside formal organizations. They become leaders because they have vision and stand up for something they believe in. Others are attracted to them, because they have charisma and inspire others by their courage and ideals. They do not seek to lead but others choose to follow them. Organizations grow up around them.

HESED AND INDIVIDUAL DEVELOPMENT

Hesed equates to the stage of our childhood when we begin to focus on the outside world. We begin to explore the limitations of our bodies, our back yards, and our parents' patience. We want to do everything, crawl over everything, and touch everything – especially forbidden fruit. We are striving to explore our abilities and to learn. Hesedic unconditional love is important to us at this time. Unless something has gone wrong we have unconditional love for our parents and our parents for us. This gives us the security to explore this large and sometimes frightening place which is our world. Not everyone receives this Hesedic boost to their sense of self-worth and confidence. Without it, we will have the sense of struggling alone that can damage us in later life. Of course, there are times when we all feel unlovable; when we all are unlovable. Unconditional parental love teaches us that our parents may sometimes dislike the things we do, but beneath that we are loveable and worthy people.

ARCHETYPES AND CREATIVITY

At the level of Hesed, there are already basic structures within material creation that are the foundation for cells, atoms, molecules, etc. as we know them. The 'building blocks' that create the bodies of living things are there. In the human psyche, the equivalents of these building blocks are certain inherited archetypal ideas that derive from what Carl Jung called the *collective unconscious*. This is a genetic inheritance and a common core of ideas found in all human beings. Archetypes are patterns or templates that tend to appear in all cultures at all times. Many modern stories that have great appeal are based around archetypal story patterns such as the fight between Dark and Light in the Star Wars series; a fight that is both external and inter-planetary, and internal within individuals. Archetypes are the building blocks of our inner world and the source from which creativity, myth and culture spring.

It is at the level of Hesed that we begin to work with creative imagination. Great art seems to come to the artist from something outside her- or himself. Something possesses us and sweeps us up. We *must* write, *must* paint, *must* sing. The words of a poem come into our dream and wake us. We *must* write them down and they flow forth in a complete poem that needs little revision. Those who are in touch with the collective unconscious are in interior dialogue with archetypal images that sometimes seem to possess them. The frenzy of creative activity can also come to the scientist. We are all familiar with the image of the person who is obsessively trying to solve a mathematical equation or a scientific problem. All worldly considerations – the needs of the body, the needs of partners, children, parents and friends – are sacrificed by an intellect that is totally absorbed. However, this absorption is not quite the same as the creative one. It is an obsession of the mind for closure – to solve the insoluble problem. The creative obsession is an obsession to express the inexpressible – all human love, passion, and longing.

Those who would be artists must be in touch with something that is greater than they are. True artistry is a path of self-sacrifice. A connection is made via Tiferet, the altar of sacrifice, to greater considerations than those of our individual selves. True artists feel that they are instruments through which the artistic force is expressing itself. They have become priestesses or priests of Hesed.

HESED AS VISION

All visionaries partake of Hesedic consciousness. They see beyond the normal human framework, which is bounded by convention and cultural conditioning. There is a close connection between Hesed and Hod, the sefirah of the rational mind. Hesedic thinking often comes in symbolic form and transcends the mind's normal categories. It was this level of thinking that helped scientists such as Einstein to break the boundaries of his scientific training. New forms of art and science are born in Hesedic consciousness. Hesedic consciousness is not just personal, but transpersonal. At this level human minds communicate with each other on an unconscious level. It is noticeable that scientific breakthroughs often happen in different places at the same time. This gives rise to disputes about ownership and originality. What has happened is that human collective knowledge has advanced to a certain stage and the new development is the next logical step – and one that is realized by more than one person. We all draw on the collective store of human knowledge and this inspires new ideas.

SPIRITUAL EXPERIENCE OF HESED

The spiritual experience of Hesed is called the 'Vision of Love'. This can come to us at the most unexpected and unlikely times. Psychiatrist Dr. Viktor Frankl in his famous book on his experiences in Nazi concentration camps – *Man's Search for Meaning* – described how when marching to work in the early morning in a bitterly cold wind, he thought of his wife who had been imprisoned in another camp. He was transfixed by the thought that love is the ultimate and the highest goal to which humankind can aspire. Even though he was in a situation where everything material had been taken from him, the power to love had not. In contemplating the image of his wife, he was filled with a love that took him to the heights of bliss. In this place of desolation, where all was barrenness, sterility, hate and despair, the Vision of Love came like a Divine grace to sustain him. From somewhere he seemed to hear a victorious 'Yes' in answer to his question about whether human existence had an ultimate purpose.

> *At that moment a light was lit in a distant farmhouse, which stood on the horizon as if painted there, in the midst of the miserable grey dawning morning in Bavaria. 'Et lux in tenebris lucet' – and the light shineth in the darkness.*[3]

Viktor Frankl saw the light appearing in the farmhouse as a symbolic answer to his question. What he experienced was a moment which Carl Jung called 'synchronicity'. Two simultaneous events occur that are connected meaningfully to one another. To someone else, the events may seem coincidental or unconnected, but at a deeper level of our psyche we *know* that they are. This is Hesedic consciousness where everything is in intimate contact with everything else. Everything that we think and do is fed into the collective mind and can be a source of growth and healing, or a source of negativity and hate. Thus we must take responsibility for our thoughts, words, feelings and deeds.

MORAL CHOICE

At Hesed, we begin to act on the basis of the knowledge of good and evil that we acquire at Daat. At this level we can make ethical choices. We know evil, but we do not need to succumb to it. Nevertheless, we are tainted by it. Its potential is within us as part of our human heritage. The Divine could act to prevent us committing wrongdoing and harm, but It does not. It is like a parent with adolescent children who must go their own way at times in order to find their limitations and ideas of right and wrong. The parental tie must be cut and the Divine must watch Its creatures stand or fall.

Humankind has made a choice – to attempt the difficult task of evolving to Godhead – and the Divine Will permits us to try. Much misery and suffering results. We err and err again, but the Divine forgives. Kabbalah teaches us that we are made in the image of the Divine. Moses Cordovero in the *Palm Tree of Deborah* taught that we should seek to resemble the Divine. One of the greatest qualities of the Divine that we must seek to emulate is mercy. Despite its anti-Semitic bias, Shakespeare's play *The Merchant of Venice* focuses on Hesedic qualities. In the famous court room scene, Shakespeare has his heroine Portia say:

> *The quality of mercy is not strain'd,*
> *it droppeth as the gentle rain from heaven*
> *upon the place beneath: it is twice blest;*
> *it blesseth him that gives and him that takes:*
> *'tis mightiest in the mightiest: it becomes*
> *the throned monarch better than his crown;*
> *his sceptre shows the force of temporal power,*
> *the attribute to awe and majesty,*
> *wherein doth sit the dread and fear of kings;*
> *but mercy is above this sceptred sway;*

it is enthroned in the hearts of kings,
it is an attribute to God himself;
and earthly power doth then show likest God's
when mercy seasons justice.

Here we have a perfect expression of the balance necessary between Mercy and Severity, Hesed and the next sefirah of Gevurah. Shakespeare himself may have known something of Kabbalah through his knowledge of the Western Mystery Tradition. Enthusiasts of the theory that magician Sir Francis Bacon was the real author of Shakespeare's plays are keen to point to the playwright's knowledge of Kabbalah as proof.

HESEDIC QUALITIES

In Daat, humankind acquires free will. Hesed is where we can begin to exercise that free will. Hesed is connected with the power of moral choice, for which free will is an essential prerequisite. The highest morality is to practise the virtue of Hesed, which is obedience to the evolutionary will of the universe. This is not the same as obedience to human-made laws and rules that are the product of cultural conditions. This is obedience to the imperative urge of life itself, which is to be, to do, to grow and to love. The law of the universe is love. If we follow the way of loving compassion, seeking to make manifest the highest and the best within us, whatever that may be, and we do our work in the world worthily and well, then we live in accordance with the 'yes' principle – a reaching out to embrace the universe. This brings us to the realm of duty, obligation and responsibility. Human beings have been given the precious gift of consciousness and we have a duty to decide what best to do with it.

Viktor Frankl learned from his concentration camp experiences that we must learn and teach others that what matters is not what we expect from life, but what life expects from us. This is not contemplation on a mountaintop, but action within the world. With the experience of Hesed, we say, 'Yes,' to the world and enter into the work of incarnation. The work of incarnation is to make manifest the Divine in us and in the world. To do this work is to experience Absolute Love. We find this love through fulfilling our responsibilities to ourselves and to one another. We find this love through choosing our life tasks and entering into them with the fullness of our being.

Hesed is the sefirah of religious authority. In esoteric terms, Hesed is considered to be the sefirah of the Keepers – teachers on the spiritual plane who guide humankind and try to protect us from our worst excesses: a tricky task. The vice of Hesed is that prime religious vice – hypocrisy. The path of a religious leader is a difficult one and many succumb to the 'vices' of Hesed. Unable to live up to the high ideals of the religious teaching, human teachers and leaders resort to preaching one thing while practising another. Hesed is the source of moral codes and teachings that arise when devout and inspired people come close to the Divine and then try to translate their experience into a way of life for others. The difficulty, of course, is that true morality comes from living in accord with Divine will and being. Living a moral life will not in itself bring us into contact with the Divine. For this, we need love. We can follow a particular code faithfully but still fail to *feel* the appropriate emotions or to achieve a state of consciousness that makes our spiritual practice more than an empty show. Thus we return to the Hesedic vice of hypocrisy. An antidote to hypocrisy is one of the qualities associated with Hesed's planetary ruler in the Western Mystery Tradition – Jupiter. Jupiter is also known as Jove and gives us our word joviality. Keeping a sense of proportion and being able to laugh at oneself are important life skills. A lovely Hesedic image is that of the Chinese laughing Buddha and one way of knowing a true spiritual teacher is that she or he can laugh at her- or himself.

EXPLORING HESED

Below are some exercises to help you bring the energy of Hesed into your life.

EXERCISE 1: DEVELOPING YOUR CREATIVITY

If you read about the lives of writers or artists, they have one thing in common – time and space. In order to be creative, we need times of silence, when we can be alone to listen to the voice of the unconscious. All the exercises in this book mention that we need some personal space such as a quiet room in which to do the exercises. This conveys the importance of these periods of quiet communion with the unconscious and with the Divine. Many people will groan in despair at this point. They are never alone or free of the voices of small children, television, CD, traffic, etc. Solitariness, like the silence of Binah, can seem an impossible luxury. However, in order to grow, we do need to find some time for ourselves. This may be when children have gone to bed, in the early morning before children or partner wake up, or even some snatched moments during our lunch break when we go to the park. These are the points in our lives when we can turn inwards to hear the voice of the Self and to connect ourselves to the energies of the collective unconscious – a deeper layer of our psyches that is below consciousness awareness and communicates through intuition and image.

In the Western Mystery Tradition, the tarot card of the Hermit rules the path on the Tree of Life between Tiferet (the Self) and Hesed (Creative imagination). Again this brings us back to the need for solitude, something that has been important for spiritual seekers in all faiths and traditions. We are told of Deborah in the Old Testament that, 'she sat under the palm tree of Deborah, between Ramah and Beth-El in the hill country of Ephraim; and the children of Israel came up for her advice' (Judges 4:5). Deborah means bee, an insect we associate with busy-ness, but in this second phase of her life, after she had been a successful businesswoman, Deborah sought inner contemplation and tranquillity and through this became a wise woman. These times of tranquillity are when we can send out our thoughts to the Divine. The *Zohar*[4] teaches that if there is no call from below, there can be no response from above. The Heavens can only answer if we call.

When you need positive creative energy in your life, find a place of quiet and address your thoughts to the Divine. You can approach the Divine through prayer or meditation, or through exercises that are meditative but creative. Hesed is the sefirah of archetypes. Archetypal ideas arise here, as do symbols that help inspire new visions. One type of symbol associated with Hesed is the mandala. Hesed is the fourth sefirah and is associated with all shapes that exhibit 'fourness'. Mandalas are regularly shaped, usually of fourfold pattern, or multiples thereof, surrounded by a circle. You will see them used as meditation symbols in Tibetan Buddhism, as the basis for designs in the stained glass windows of Christian cathedrals, and in pre-Christian Celtic design. The fourfold shape within a circle is the basis for Navaho sand paintings used for healing and for rituals used in the Western Mystery Tradition. You might like to paint a simple mandala. You may have designs or colours that you would like to choose yourself, or you could make a mandala based on the four elements. At Hesed we have the potential for organic life that arises from the interaction of Air, Fire, Water and Earth.

To draw a mandala based around the four elements, take a large piece of drawing paper and some paints or coloured pens or pencils. Draw a large circle in the centre, divided into equal portions by a diagonal cross. Devote the topmost portion to the element of Air, the bottom to Water, the left to Earth and the right to Fire or Sun. Now paint or draw in each quadrant, a scene, abstract or representational, that seems to you to express the essence of the individual elements. When you have finished, you will have your own personal mandala of creation.

Feed your creativity by exposing yourself to films, music, art, literature and theatre. Try to attend at least one cultural or artistic event a month, and more if you can. Read at least one book a month. Expand your horizons. Listen to music that stretches you and buy novels recommended by critics as good examples of contemporary writing. Develop your own creativity further. Is there an activity you once enjoyed that you have given up for lack of time, such as a craft skill, painting, dance, acting, singing, or playing a musical instrument? Could you make room for it in your life once more; if not on a regular basis then once a year for a weekend or vacation away? Remember these do not have to be solitary activities. Many creative holidays can be shared with family and friends.

EXERCISE 2: BRINGING HESEDIC ENERGY INTO YOUR LIFE

At Daat we begin to acquire independence. We have our own personal life experience to draw on as well as that of our parents. Hesed is the stage when we begin to explore our world. If we have had loving and supportive families, we will enter this stage of our lives with confidence and excitement. There are new things to learn – new skills and new knowledge – and everything is open to us; the possibilities are endless. We will feel optimism, hope and confidence – all qualities associated with Hesed's planetary ruler Jupiter.

Some aspects of learning to say 'yes' rather than 'no' to the universe relate to the personality variable known as extraversion. Saying 'yes' means developing a positive and outward-looking attitude to the universe. In the Western Mystery Tradition, Hesed's planet Jupiter relates to expansion – turning outwards to the universe and seeing what it has to offer. Here are some ideas to help you develop your Hesedic qualities:

- If people ask you about your achievements, tell them. This is not boasting.
- If a new opportunity presents itself, try it.
- If you want to contact someone, make the first move. Reach out to people. In other words, become a prime mover, someone who makes things happen.
- If there is an activity you would like to happen but no one is organizing it, organize it yourself. Take the lead.
- If there is a far-off place you have always wanted to visit, visit it. Travel and broaden your horizons.

The main magical colour associated with Jupiter is bright blue like a summer sky. When you want Hesedic energy around you, bring this colour into your life. Amethyst is the stone of Jupiter. This is a cheap and affordable stone. You can keep a piece of amethyst in your pocket, or wear it in the form of a necklace or ring. Wear amethyst when you are starting out on a new venture and/or when you want confidence and good luck. Wear it to job interviews. Put a piece on or in your office desk.

In the Western Magical Tradition, Hesed is a water sefirah on the Pillar of Force or Fire. Water plus fire equals warm water. When you want Hesedic energy, go to the sea on a warm day, or have a warm bath or a steam bath. Warmth relaxes our limbs and makes us feel expansive. It stops us being 'uptight'. Massage is a useful adjunct to all this. It releases tension and tightness in the muscles.

Hesed is a sefirah of loving-kindness or altruism. Altruism means doing something for others without expectation of direct reward. I say 'direct reward' because we do not do things unless we get some kind of positive feedback. That feedback might be the pleasure of seeing another's smile, it might be the knowledge that we are contributing something to alleviate world poverty, it might be the satisfaction that we have given something back to the world. Make altruistic giving part of your life. It does not have to be a dominant force and it is best done quietly and secretly. If you give, you will receive. People will respond to you differently if they sense you are an outward-looking person who is concerned about others.

TO GEVURAH

Hesed is a force for change. Hesed brings new ideas and visions of how things should be and gives people the inspiration to see what must be done. Hesed alone will not do it however. Hesed's vision must be accompanied by the courage of Gevurah. Let us now turn to Gevurah.

Hesed – Mercy

Titles: Gedulah – Love, Majesty, Magnificence
Image: A mighty monarch

Divine Aspect

Hebrew Divine Name: *El* – Mighty One
Deities in other traditions: Shepherd Gods, ruler Gods, the Chinese laughing Buddha (not strictly a God but treated as such), Ganesh (the laughing elephant-headed God who is son of the supreme deity Brahma)
Spiritual Paths: The Bodhisattva path in Mahayana Buddhism, aspects of Kabbalah and Christianity

Correspondences in the Physical Universe

In the Cosmos: Tzadekh – Jupiter
Number: 4
Colour: Blue

Correspondences in Humankind

Spiritual experience: Vision of Love
Positive quality: Obedience
Negative qualities: Tyranny, hypocrisy, bigotry, gluttony
In the human body: the left arm and shoulder, which is nearest to the heart and has shed no one's blood, the shield arm

Notes

1. Cordovero (1588) Chapter I, Attributes 1–2.
2. Jung (1961, page 387). Written towards the end of his life.
3. Frankl (1984 ed., pages 51–2).
4. *Zohar* 3:164a.

5

GEVURAH – POWER OR SEVERITY

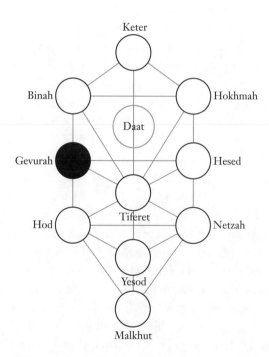

The fifth path is called 'Rooted Consciousness' (Sekhel Nishrash),
because it is more akin than any other to the Supreme Unity.
It is unified in the essence of Understanding (Binah),
which emanates from the depths of the original Wisdom (Hokhmah).
SEFER YETZIRAH

At Hesed the Divine begins to create pattern, shape and ideas. At Gevurah, the Divine decides which of the many creative possibilities It has generated will manifest in this cycle of creation. This is an ongoing process that ends only when this cosmos collapses in on itself before a new phase of creation begins.

THE DIVINE IN GEVURAH

The Hebrew Divine name in Gevurah is *Elohim Givor*, Gods or Goddesses and Gods of Strength. Gevurah is associated with war. It is no accident that the headquarters of the United States' military machine is the Pentagon. Many of the early founders of the United States were Freemasons and members of magical orders who understood the power of symbolism. In designing a building to house a military headquarters, the United States chose a shape that was associated with war. This is a five-sided figure – the pentagon – symbolic of the fifth sefirah – Gevurah. War in this context is considered to be a force of good and a check on evil. It is an exercise in restructuring and pruning – of cutting out diseased growth so that new healthy growth can replace it. Gevurah brings endings but also the possibility of new beginnings. It is like the forest fire that destroys the old timber but allows new growth to spring up. The speed at which new growth does spring up after a forest fire is one of the wonders of nature.

We tend to think of war as a masculine pursuit, but Gevurah is traditionally a feminine sefirah. The Semitic Goddess associated with war is Anat, who in the early days of the Israelites was worshipped as the wife of Yahweh/Jehovah. She did not make or start war, but she could be invoked to win it. The ancient Egyptian lioness-headed Goddess Sekhmet is another Gevuric war Goddess, although she is also a Tiferetic Goddess of healing. In the Western Mystery Tradition, this is the realm of the battle Goddesses, such as the Morrigan of Irish tradition and the Valkyries of the Norse. It is also the realm of Goddesses of destruction. In Binah we have the weaver Goddesses, but in Gevurah we have the executioner Goddesses – those that cut the thread of life. Binah is associated with death and Gevurah with the killing that is one passageway to death.

Death and destruction must always seem negative to those that experience them, but the cycle of new life and growth demands that we discard that which is outworn. When the human body decays beyond its viability, we experience death and separation from the body. Figures from myth, fairy tale and folklore such as the Grim Reaper partake of the nature of Gevurah. Gevurah is the quality control mechanism of creation. She is constantly checking the forms she creates and discarding those that are unsuitable. Gevurah helps dispose of evil. What is imbalanced, unnecessary and antagonistic to cosmic harmony is thrown into the abyss that lies at the feet of Binah the Great Mother.

TITLES AND IMAGES

Two of Gevurah's titles are *Pachad*, which means fear, and *Din*, which means Justice. Often, of course, fear is aroused by the operations of justice. Gevurah is associated with Karma and with reaping what we sow. This is not always a pleasant experience: humankind has much to answer for. One image of Gevurah is of a Warrior Queen or King riding in a Chariot. The tarot card of the Chariot, which is associated with the path of the Tree of Life descending from Binah to Gevurah, is such an image. Gevurah also sends us messages from the collective unconscious, as does Hesed. Here they are less likely to be creative ideas and more likely to be warnings and premonitions of death and disaster. Gevurah is about destruction but if we understand Gevurah, we can see certain trends and tides and can seek to avert them.

GEVURAH AND LEADERSHIP

Hesed is the sefirah of the religious leader and guru. Gevurah by way of contrast is the sefirah of military, business and political leadership. Gevurah gives us the qualities of planning and concentration and the ability to organize large resources. This type of organizational ability is important for those who run large modern institutions such as governments and business corporations. The qualities required for the successful operation of a modern business in a competitive world overlap with those of the hunter and warrior. Running a successful business requires a clear focus, goals and purpose. Those who run governments need the same mindset. It is one that sees beyond the difficulties and is not daunted. This is Gevurah.

SPIRITUAL EXPERIENCE OF GEVURAH

The spiritual experience of Gevurah is the Vision of Power. Those who experience this vision can be forces of great good – or great evil. All great leaders have an understanding of the nature of power and how to wield it. Margaret Thatcher was a Gevuric personality who identified what she saw as wrong in British society – powerful trade unions which she perceived as promoting their members' interests above those of their country. She decided to break their power and became known as the 'Iron Lady', an appropriate title as iron is a metal associated in the Western Mystery Tradition with Gevurah. One of the problems of Gevurah is the heady wine of self-righteousness. Gevuric energy can be an infection that takes over the psyche and obliterates reason. We talk quite rightly about being 'drunk with power' and such is the fate of those who wield it too long or too successfully.

To have the Vision of Power, we must feel *empowered*. We must feel in control of our own lives. This is one of the qualities of a mature adult personality. Many people do not feel in control of their lives. Control is one of the functions of Gevurah. We can never be completely in control of our lives. We all know 'control freaks' who try to be 'on top of everything', and to 'have everything at their finger tips'. Such people are a nightmare to work with. They cannot delegate and will not allow others the same autonomy they demand for themselves. To attempt to control everything and everyone leads to one of the vices of Hesed, tyranny. To attempt to control nothing is to fail in our Gevuric duty of taking responsibility for ourselves. Between the competing energies of Hesed and Gevurah, we must find a point of balance.

GEVURAH AND INDIVIDUAL DEVELOPMENT

Gevurah is the stage in our individual development when we start to encounter the rules and regulations of our societies. We have to venture forth from the shelter of the parental home and enter the world of school and education. We begin to discover our limitations and begin to learn to focus on doing what we are good at. We start to take control of what we do and we begin to learn to deal with our emotions. We have to learn discipline and to conform to the often unwelcome structures of others – with class timetables that prevent us from playing and make us do things we do not want to do. We have to learn to postpone what we want. We learn that certain behaviours and sets of conduct are required of us. The pressures come not only from teachers, but also from our peer group, other children. In the playground we learn that we have to conform if we want to be accepted. We have to learn self-control and to suppress our anger and impetuosity in order to fit in with Gevurah's demands and boundaries.

Gevurah is about exercising Din, judgement. We must judge our actions and ourselves. We must also learn to rely on our own judgement and to take responsibility for our own lives. For the first part of our lives, others such as parents and teachers take decisions for us. As we grow, it is important that we begin to make our own decisions.

GEVURIC QUALITIES

The virtues or positive aspects of Gevurah are energy and courage. Gevurah represents the rigours of existence. By developing energy and courage to overcome obstacles that challenge us, we develop and grow. Gevuric experiences often teach us that certain ways of being, or doing, are not adequate in the new situation. We have to change and evolve. Reality is that we live in a changing universe and we must accept that we cannot hang on to anything in this world, be it power, position or worldly wealth. It is important to remember that all form is temporary. Life and the Divine force are continually moving forward and seeking new forms.

Energy and courage are related to another positive quality of Gevurah –

will. The concept of Will was particularly important in the psychologies of two Jewish psychotherapists, Alfred Adler, founder of the social psychiatry movement, and Roberto Assagioli, founder of psychosynthesis. The energy of Gevurah is one of our primary driving forces. When it is in balance with the energies of the other sefirot, Gevurah becomes will in the sense of energy and 'Will to Act'. Gevurah, when harnessed, becomes the power to overcome inertia. It becomes the energy and conviction that allow us to strive for right and to build a better society. Gevurah gives us the will to achieve our true aims. Roberto Assagioli had a wide knowledge of spiritual traditions. He was familiar with the Judaism of his birth and he also studied Eastern religions and the esoteric and magical systems of the West. His spiritual studies were important in developing his concept of will. In his book *The Act of Will*, he described six stages necessary for the complete and effective expression of the will:

1. Goal, valuation, motivation
2. Deliberation
3. Decision
4. Affirmation
5. Planning
6. Direction of the execution

These stages epitomize the organized approach of harnessed Gevuric energy. Goal relates to Tiferet, the sefirah that follows Gevurah. Gevurah works well when committed to a balanced purpose. Assagioli also believed that by developing our wills we could transmute unchannelled sexual and aggressive energies. This would cause an awakening, release and employment of potent spiritual energies, which can transform and regenerate the personality. A beautiful book in this context is Piero Ferrucci's *What We May Be*. Ferrucci had a doctorate in philosophy and education and became involved in psychology through Laura Huxley, wife of Aldous Huxley, whom he met in the United States when visiting in 1969. In 1970 he went to Florence to work with Roberto Assagioli and collaborated closely with him until Assagioli's death in 1974. Assagioli taught Ferrucci that for human beings to be happy, we must take into account all aspects of human life, including the spiritual. If some parts of life are left unacknowledged, we lead fragmented, even absurd existences. The dimensions he saw as important included:

the realization of love [Hesed]
the emergence of will and self-determination [Gevurah]
the awakening of intuition [Tiferet]
the enjoyment of beauty [Netzah]
the sharpening of the mind [Hod]
and the enrichment of the imagination [Yesod]
the discovery of the Self and its purpose [Malkhut and the journey of return].

LOVE AND WILL

Hesed is about love and saying, 'Yes'. It is associated with giving. Gevurah is about judgement and saying, 'No'. It is about withholding. Hesed is essentially libertarian. This can translate into permissiveness that allows evil and denies the ability to choose. Hesed can be cultural relativism where we deny our own set of values. Gevurah is the counterbalancing tendency. In its positive aspect, Gevurah is the ability to choose and to exercise free will; that dearly bought gift of Daat. After his experiences in concentration camps during the Second World War, what impressed Viktor Frankl most of all was that despite the terrible conditions under which people lived – the deprivation, starvation, cruelty and constant fear of death – it was still possible to exercise free will. The concentration camp inmates were imprisoned physically, but there was still in their daily actions the possibility of choice. There was the choice to help one another or not. They had the choice to love or hate; to endure and hope, or to despair. One of humankind's greatest assets is our ability to hold on to a sense of individual identity in the most adverse conditions. This makes us go on, when logically it seems we should despair. Here the spiritual experience of Gevurah – the Vision of Power – is a Vision of Empowerment. Gevurah teaches us that everything depends on the stance we take with regard to our experiences. Viktor Frankl found that even in the most terrible conditions, the human mind was more than the product of our biology, physiology or social conditioning. Indwelling within us is a Divine spirit that enables us to exercise our will. Frankl noted that every day there were opportunities to exercise the power of choice – to submit to degradation or to maintain one's inner spirit unbowed; to share with others or to be selfish; to give or to take. Gevurah's lesson is that life is a precious gift and we are responsible for living it as well as we can. For Viktor Frankl, the meaning of life was in living up to its demands and expectations. The Divine Oneness has expectations of us. It has created us, each individual one of us, with a purpose. Our goal in life is to seek to know that purpose and to do it.

An important truth is that we create our own environment. Just as we have free will from Hesed and the power to say 'yes' to the universe; so too do we have the power to refuse evil. There is a wonderful Buddhist gesture that consists of raising the right hand palm outwards. This is a gesture of refusal of evil; to say that such and such must not be, we must act. Great heroes who have braved the tide of conventional opinion to do good fall into this mould. People such as Oskar Schindler and Raoul Wallenberg saved hundreds of Jews from Nazi persecution, strangers who were little known to them, simply because they perceived that what was happening was wrong. This is not to forget Frau Schindler who had to find thousands of meals to feed the people her husband had so generously rescued – a truly Gevuric miracle of organization. These people are not holy people in a conventional sense but they are heroes who dared do what others did not. Gevurah is the realm of heroines and heroes.

RATIONALIZATION

Hesed is a forward movement in the psyche. It is a progressive movement outward. Gevurah is the opposite. It is when we say, 'Hey, hold on. Is this a good idea? Let's stop and think. Maybe we need to refine our strategy here.' Hesed give us vision, Gevurah helps us put our ideas into practice. Hesed, the creative department of the universe, constantly imagines new possibilities and forms in which the Divine life force can manifest Itself. Gevurah is the implementation team. It is the reality principle against which Hesed's visions must be measured. What is practical? What will work? What fits in with other greater and larger plans? Gevurah must tailor visions to fit.

Gevurah in corporate terms is rationalization and downsizing. Perhaps an organization goes through a period of growth and acquisition. In its acquisitions it buys companies that turn out to have subsidiaries that do not fit the core aims of the main business. Perhaps they are not as profit making; perhaps they are in a declining market, or maybe they are just too divergent in their products and markets to make a rational coherent whole with the rest. This is where Gevuric company directors will sit down and rationalize, 'Let's sell off this and wind down that.' Redundancies come. Laying off loyal workers is hard, but the Gevuric manager will say that this must be done to protect the rest. In the same way, the Gevuric general will sacrifice some lives in order to save others. The Gevuric gardener will prune back the roses so that they may grow more strongly the next season.

THE SHADOW OF RATIONALITY

Reason is a powerful force but, like all powerful forces, it has its Shadow side. We live in a world often dominated by negative emotions justified by reason. War and inter-group hate, the Shadow side of Gevurah, draw some of their energy through a resonance between Gevurah and Netzah. Netzah is emotion on the individual level. Gevurah is emotion on the group level. Gevurah appears to be the epitome of the rationality of the modern bureaucratic state, but Gevuric energies are aroused by primitive animalistic emotions of approach–avoidance. In Gevurah we have avoidance. We have fear and mistrust of those who are 'other' or in some way different from ourselves. People of different races, sexual orientation, or those with bodies that are 'different' because of disability, are seen as frightening and threatening. There is a dreadful rationality in Gevurah, in service of what are essentially emotional drives. These are the forces that made ordinary people work out railway timetables that would most effectively transport people to concentration camps, charging only the guards the return fare.

SHADOW AND GEVURAH

From Binah onwards, the emanation of any sefirah can appear good or evil depending on the circumstances in which we find ourselves. To the rationalist, the cold logic of Gevurah is good. Try telling that to someone in the throes of their first love. In the *Zohar*, Divine mercy is partnered by Divine severity. One must balance the other. The *Zohar*[1] says that the Divine, in creating the world, meant it to be based on justice. However, human nature is so flawed that if we were all treated with justice untempered by mercy, humankind would be in a sorry state.

The Shadow exists for all the sefirot in the form of negative qualities associated with the energy of the sefirah as it manifests in the psychological realm. However, we may find it easier to recognize the Shadow in Gevurah because when Gevurah's energy is misused the consequences are severe. In fact, the greatest of human tragedies and disasters have been caused by the misuse of Gevuric force. This is the negative, undeveloped and unevolved side of the personality. A problem with the Shadow in the human psyche is that we have difficulty in recognizing our own negative impulses. Much of our negative behaviour is unconscious – we are not even aware that we are doing it. The psychologist Carl Jung wrote[2] that human beings are, unfortunately, much less good than they imagine themselves to be. The more unaware we are of our Shadow, the blacker and denser it will be. The more dissociated it is from our conscious life, the more it will display a compensatory demonic dynamism.

The Shadow operates in a peculiar way. We cannot recognize its qualities in ourselves, but we do recognize those qualities in others. The Shadow is often at work when we meet someone for the first time and instinctively dislike him or her. It might just be that he or she is a nasty, unpleasant person. However, it may be that unconsciously you see in this person something that you do not like in yourself. The Shadow also operates in another way. If we have qualities in ourselves that we do not like, we may project them onto other individuals and social groups. These are then thought to embody all the immature, evil, and other repressed tendencies that are hidden in our own psyches. This is an important factor in racial prejudice. When we project our negative qualities onto others, we live in a dangerous world, because it is an illusionary one. We see things in others that are not there – negative things – and this arouses Gevuric energy within us.

There are people who see only the negative side of life. Everyone is bad; everything is bad. These are the people who start moral crusades to purge people of their wrongs. They become dangerous fanatics and Gevurah is the sefirah of the fanatic. The urge is to exterminate that which is hateful. We try and destroy those that represent for us all the hateful qualities that we despise. And of course, we cannot succeed. The hateful qualities that we are trying to extinguish are hidden within us. Our quest is hopeless. Whole societies can project their negativity onto others – Christians and Jews, Jews and Moslems, Moslems and Christians, Serbs and Albanians, Catholics and Protestants. Projection also occurs on an individual level. This is the fantasy of the serial killer who considers himself chosen by God to exterminate individuals who represent for him all that is wrong with the world. The Shadow has its own aims and goals and can act in spite of our conscious will. How often do we say, 'I don't know what made me do that!' when it is our own 'dark twin' that is operating? This does not mean that Gevurah is a negative sefirah but that this is the negative side of Gevurah.

The Shadow is not wholly negative. The Shadow represents all that we try to repress about ourselves. It has a will of its own and can manifest in all sorts of negative behaviour. However, a positive effect of the Shadow's emergence is that it gives us an opportunity to recognize what is happening. The Shadow is a term that has emerged from modern psychology but the concept is a traditional Kabbalistic one. Moses Cordovero taught that we create a 'destroying angel' whenever we do wrong, a 'prosecutor', 'who stands before the Blessed Holy One saying: "So-and-so made me".'[3] This archaic language is alien to us, but what is Moses Cordovero saying in modern terms? He means that we create a voice within when do what we know consciously or unconsciously to be wrong. This is the conscience that tells us what we do not want to know. We try to suppress the unpleasant reality, but it cannot be suppressed. There is something within us that drives towards realization. The divine part of ourselves wants us to triumph over our negativity and the Shadow side of ourselves lures us into exposing it, even if we do not wish to do so. This is where the Shadow can be our friend. It helps us unmask hypocrisy (the vice of the sefirah of Hesed) and to see the truth.

ADULT RESPONSIBILITY

Gevurah is the stage of development at which the over-enthusiastic mistakes of Hesed are rectified. It is associated with Karma and with taking active responsibility for the consequences of our actions. Taking responsibility for all our actions, both good and bad, is one of the tests of a mature adult personality. It is taught by good parenting, education, and example. We learn early on that sometimes even our best intentions go wrong. Errors are a necessary part of living. We cannot escape them and must learn to own them. It is also important to understand that we are all interconnected through the collective unconscious. We are also responsible for the actions of other members of our species and what one of us is capable of, so are others, if only in part.

When we consider the personalities of those who commit great evil, we do discover psychopaths, but these are not the usual perpetrators of evil deeds. Great evil is committed by the most ordinary and insignificant of people. The moral philosopher Hannah Arendt coined the term the 'Banality of Evil' in 1961 when she was sent to report on the trial of Adolf Eichmann, the SS officer who installed the Auschwitz gas chambers and made sure that 'production' targets were met in order to please his Führer. Eichmann had no personal animosity towards Jews. He was a former low-grade sales representative rumoured to have had a Jewish mistress. However, he did love to obey orders. Brought up by an authoritarian father, who beat him, in a home where his mother died early on, young Adolf learned to obey those above him. While awaiting trial in Israel for his crimes, Eichmann wrote in his memoirs.

> *I recognized my father, and my mother who died early, as absolute authority. I acknowledged teachers and later professional bosses as authority, and even later, military and service supervisors.*[4]

The ability to evade moral responsibility by placing the responsibility for our actions on others is a dangerous and slippery slope. Eichmann himself later admitted:

Today, 15 years after 8 May 1945, I know ... that a life of obedience, led by orders, instructions, decrees and directives, is a very comfortable one in which one's creative thinking is diminished.[5]

Eichmann was as much led by obedience, the virtue or positive quality of Hesed, as by the vice of Gevurah, cruelty. It is important to remember that once we move beyond Hokhmah, nothing is pure. Obedience to the wrong authority leads to evil. Obedience must be to humanitarian ideals rather than to human organizations. Eichmann was also the epitome of the Authoritarian Personality. The term comes from a six-year project funded by the United States government in 1944 and conducted by Theodore Adorno to identify the types of individuals who could get sucked into the Nazi mindset. Two major personality dimensions emerged – authoritarianism and ethnocentrism. High regard for and tendency to acquiesce to authority, adherence to conventional middle-class values, rigidity in thinking, and need for clear structure, characterized authoritarianism. Ethnocentrism was defined by loyalty to one's own group and distrust and dislike of members of other groups. These are the dangers when Gevurah energizes the negative qualities of Hesed. Hannah Arendt concluded in her book *Eichmann in Jerusalem: A Report on the Banality of Evil* that Eichmann became a mass murderer because he failed to exercise critical thought. He did not question what he did. The power of critical thought is a saving grace of Gevurah. It gives us the energy and courage to say, 'No.'

EXPLORING GEVURAH

EXERCISE 1: ENERGIZING YOURSELF

This is an exercise to help you focus on the Divine in Gevurah – Elohim Givor. Focusing on different aspects of deity can help us manifest the qualities of that aspect of deity in our everyday lives. You will need about 20 minutes for this exercise.

1. Find a comfortable chair where you can sit with your spine straight, or you could sit or kneel on the floor if you prefer.
2. Relax and then visualize a column of white light pouring down over your crown.
3. The white light enters the crown of your head and flows through you. It flows down through your skull, cleansing your psyche. It flows right through you and down into the floor beneath.
4. With the flow of the white light, all negative energy is removed from you. You feel the clear, light energy of the Divine Presence filling you and uniting you with the spiritual realm.
5. The light continues to flow down through you and also over you. It is a continuous white stream without beginning and without ending. The streaming light clears out all negative thoughts. It clears out jealousy and anger. It clears out all barriers that prevent you realizing your own inner powers. It leaves you focused in the present, with a strong desire to order your life in the way in which you wish.
6. Now say an invocation to the Divine in Gevurah.

Elohim Givor, Divine Power of Strength,
Changer of what seems changeless
and Energizer of the world;
help me to find my strength, energy and power;
grant me the will to change the pattern of my existence.
Show me how my strength can unite with yours,
that I may be as you would have me be.
Amen, or So mote it be.

7. Allow the flow of light to cease. The clear sense of purpose that contact with the Divine Light has given you remains. You find that you are in your own space, with a focused energy and purpose that you can use in the days to come.
8. Repeat this exercise when you have need of focused energy.

EXERCISE 2: TRANSFORMING ANGER

Gevurah is a sefirah associated with the element of Fire. It is placed on the Pillar of Form in the Tree of Life; the Pillar associated with Water. Gevurah is therefore Fire of Water. Anger is a fiery emotion that makes us cold to others. This is the mixture of the fire and water of Gevurah. Anger is also an energetic activity. Sometimes that activity is expressed outwardly, exploding into violence. Sometimes it is contained inwardly and we seethe with anger like a bubbling cauldron, or we become inwardly cold, like ice.

This is an exercise to explore how you experience anger.

1. Think about how you express aggression.
    * Do you express it?
    * Do you erupt into violent words or actions like a fiery volcano?
    * Alternatively, do you become cold, brooding and vengeful, like an ocean before a storm?
    * Do you repress your anger, rather than expressing it?
    * Do you deny it; pretending that you never experience anger at all?
2. Try to remember the last two occasions on which you became really angry. What caused your anger? Are there particular situations that make you angry?
    * Driving in heavy traffic (road rage)
    * Crowded places (territorial anger)
    * People who pressurize you to impossible deadlines at work (anger of disempowerment)
    * Situations where people are being oppressed or abused (righteous wrath)
    * Situations where you feel demeaned or humiliated (threats to your self-esteem)?
3. The positive quality of Gevurah is energy. One way of dealing with anger is to turn it into something else. Expressing ourselves can be a channel for Gevuric energy. You could try painting, writing a story, poem, or your diary. Remember that artists are often subject to rages and easily frustrated. The anger of frustration will be released if you give it an outlet through which to express itself. Righteous wrath can be an extremely negative emotion if it remains simply that. If however

we direct the energy that makes us angry about a situation of injustice or abuse into worthwhile activity such as joining and working for an organization to help change the situation, then our anger can become a source for good. Many idealists and freedom fighters have been inspired by anger against a system of injustice. Gevurah is also associated with clearing out the outworn. When you become angry, try tidying, clearing out and cleaning your living space or your office. Go to the bottle bank – smashing all that glass is a satisfying Gevuric activity. Re-ordering your environment in a more satisfactory way will give you a sense of control and will be a useful outlet for your Gevuric energy. You start to manifest your will.

TO TIFERET

Gevuric energy is positive if balanced and negative if not. We can use our Gevuric energy wisely if we harness it to appropriate goals. Finding the goals that are right for us is part of the function of the next sefirah – Tiferet.

Gevurah – Power or Strength

Titles: Pachad – fear, Din – justice
Images: Warrior, Warrior Queen, mighty warrior in a chariot

Divine Aspect

Hebrew Divine Name: *Elohim Givor*
Deities in other traditions: Anat (Semitic goddess of war), Kali (Hindu goddess of war), the Morrigan (Irish goddess of battle), Valkyries (Norse goddesses of battle), Sekhmet (Egyptian goddess of battle)
Spiritual Paths: Martial arts, warrior cults – aspects of Odin worship in the Norse Tradition, and the cult of Mithras for Roman soldiery, Knights Templar and other spiritual military orders, aspects of Islam

Correspondences in the Physical Universe

In the Cosmos: Madim (Mars)
Number: 5
Colour: Red

Correspondences in Humankind

Spiritual Experience: Vision of Power
Positive aspect: courage and energy
Negative aspect: cruelty
In the human body: right hand and arm (the sword arm)

Notes

1. Margliot (1964 ed.) *I*, 180b.

2. Jung (1968 ed., page 131).

3. See Cordovero (1588).

4. Quoted in Imre Kazaks (August 1999), 'Memoirs of an Accidental Murderer', *Independent: Friday Review* (page 1).

5. Quoted in Imre Kazaks (August 1999), 'Memoirs of an Accidental Murderer', *Independent: Friday Review* (page 1).

6

TIFERET – BEAUTY

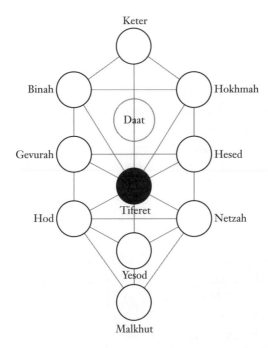

Keter

Binah

Hokhmah

Daat

Gevurah

Hesed

Hod

Tiferet

Netzah

Yesod

Malkhut

The sixth path is called 'Inflowing Intuitive Consciousness'
(Sekhel Shefa Nivdal),[1]
because the inflowing emanations increase themselves therein.
It transmits this influence to those fortunate people
who are united with it.

SEFER YETZIRAH

Tiferet is 'Beauty' or 'Harmony'. At Tiferet we come to a major balancing point of the Tree of Life. Tiferet is directly connected to, influences and is influenced by all the sefirot apart from Malkhut. Tiferet is the nerve centre of the Tree. Tiferet is associated in the Western Mystery Tradition with the Sun. Solar energy is essential for life as we know it. This is the stage in biological development when simple organisms begin to combine to create new life forms. They do so by reaching out to others different from themselves and combining and synthesizing, a function of the central column of the Tree of Life. Tiferet is like some aspects of Keter on a lower arc. It initiates a new phase in creation – the beginnings of species as we know them.

About 2,000 million years ago, eukaryotic cells began to evolve by ingesting other species of cells and, instead of digesting them, incorporated them as permanent, genetically reproducible parts of themselves. Chloroplasts, for example, act as 'engines' and enable plants to convert solar radiation into chemical energy and mitochondria process that energy in both plant and animal cells. From simple structures we moved to more complex. Complex cells with nuclei and specialized internal structures to process energy are the basis of all higher life forms – plants, fungi, animals and people.

THE DIVINE IN TIFERET

Tiferet is often spoken of as the son of Binah and Hokhmah, the Divine Feminine and the Divine Masculine. The Divine Name associated with Tiferet is Jehovah (YHVH) Eloah va Daat, which we can translate as 'Divine All-Knowing One'. YHVH's four letters are known as the Tetragrammaton. The four Hebrew letters are Yod, He, Vau, He. Traditionally *Yod* is associated with Hokhmah and is considered to represent the Father. *He* represents the Mother or Binah. *Vau* represents the Son of Binah and Hokhmah, who is described either as Tiferet, or as all the six sefirot from Hesed through to Yesod. The second *He* represents the tenth sefirah, the Daughter, Malkhut, who is also known as the Shekhinah, the Bride of the Son. Kabbalah frequently talks of Tiferet and Malkhut as Bridegroom and Bride. The point at which Tiferet and Malkhut join is Yesod, Foundation. Yesod is associated in the body with the penis. Thus, Tiferet and Malkhut are joined by a sacred marriage that results in the final stage of the Divine entering matter. The name YHVH therefore represents all the aspects of the Divine that have manifested out of Keter.

The incorporation of the word 'Daat' in Jehovah Eloah va Daat suggests that Tiferet has access to the knowledge of the mysterious Daat. Tiferet is intimately associated with Daat. At Tiferet we can draw on not only our personal knowledge but also the knowledge of the collective repository of human memory – the collective unconscious. At Tiferet we stand on four boundaries – those of the human conscious mind, the human personal unconscious, the human collective unconscious and Divine cosmic consciousness.

The Divine in Tiferet can reach out and communicate with humankind. This is the realm where the human and Divine meet. This is the sefirah of the Messiah, who acts as both political and religious leader, and combines the energy of Gevurah and Hesed. In other traditions it is the sefirah of saviour deities, such as Christ (whose image is partly based on ancient archetypes and partly on an historical personage's life), and the Egyptian Goddess Isis as she was worshipped in the Graeco-Egyptian era as Supreme deity of humankind.

It is important to understand that sefirot which are 'lower down' the Tree are not less evolved states of consciousness. In fact, Malkhut, the Kingdom, is the highest expression of Divine creative force. Tiferetic consciousness is therefore more evolved than that of Gevurah or Hesed. Ideally, it combines the qualities of both. We can envisage this better if we turn the Tree horizontally (remembering that in the spiritual realm, notions such as 'up', 'down', 'along', are only metaphors).

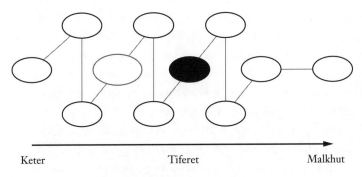

Keter   Tiferet   Malkhut

Horizontal Tree of Life

Tiferet draws together the forces of the first five sefirot and brings their energies to manifest in matter.

Tiferet is the realm of moral awareness. We have the powers of Love (Hesed) and Will (Gevurah) and in Tiferet we have conscious awareness and the ability to exercise the qualities of Hesed and Gevurah. Of course, the ability to exercise these qualities depends on having a clear heart and mind. We must be centred – aware of the Divine Will that precedes the emergence of our own and the needs of the material world in which we must exercise our moral choices and live with the consequences.

HEALTH AND HEALING

The Divine in Tiferet operates from the point of harmony. It is therefore a healing energy and is associated in the Western Mystery Tradition with healing deities, such as Egyptian Sekhmet, who is a Goddess of healing as well as of war and is known as the beloved daughter of the Sun God Ra. When rose grower and healer Lionel Poole offered to breed for Britain's National Federation of Spiritual Healers a special rose with the name 'Healing Hands',[2] he and the Federation chose a pale yellow rose tinged with pink – a combination of the colours of Tiferet. Unconsciously, people often use Kabbalistic symbolism even if they are not Kabbalists because Kabbalah represents an accumulated storehouse of knowledge, wisdom and symbol that is lodged deeply in the Western psyche. If you think about Tiferet as a place of harmony and beauty, the association with healing, which is when the body is in harmony, is obvious.

Health is an important gift of the Divine and we need to treasure it. The *Bahir* teaches that if someone does not act with Kindness (Hesed) towards him- or herself, he or she cannot be called Hasid (pious).[3] For true health, we must be healthy in body, mind and spirit. Tiferet is the sefirah of psychosomatic diseases. By this we do not mean imaginary diseases, but diseases that spring from deep wounds to the Self. Cancer and many other diseases are physical diseases that can be triggered by emotional trauma such as bereavement. A deep sorrow (Binah) caused by death may cause the body to turn against itself (Gevurah) in an unconscious longing for death, which then manifests in the body as illnes. Often we take good health for granted and it is only when confronted with the illness of others that we realize the vulnerability of our own bodies. Kabbalah teaches that we have a responsibility to look after our bodies, which are temples of the spirit.

TITLES AND IMAGES

Tiferet is known as *Melekh*, the King, and as *Zoar Anpin*, an Aramaic term meaning Lesser Countenance or Short Face. This is in contrast with the *Arikh Anpin* of Keter – the 'Greater Countenance' or 'Long Face'. Tiferet and the sefirot from Hesed to Yesod are also sometimes called The Impatient One. These are all attempts to convey in symbolic language the idea that Keter is long-suffering about the follies of humankind, but that Tiferet and its surrounding sefirot are less tolerant.

Tiferet is often referred to as the Son. Gods who are sons are found in all the Near and Middle Eastern fertility myths and Christianity drew on these. Thus Christ, Tammuz and Adonis are all deities who are sons who never become fathers and who are eventually sacrificed and reborn. An image strongly associated with Tiferet is that of the Son of the Great Mother crucified upon the Tree. We find this imagery in the Near Eastern deities Attis and Cybele, and in Christ and the Virgin Mary. Further north, a similar image is found in Norse myth, where the God Odin is hung upon the World Tree. In the earlier myths, the Sacred Son was closely associated with the green and growing vegetation. His sacrifice ensured the renewal of each year's cycle of fertility and growth. In the more complex Christian myth, the sacrifice of the son is to ensure the renewal and rebirth of humankind. It awakens humankind to a new state of consciousness. Odin's sacrifice is not that of a vegetation king who renews the Earth, or of Christ who renews humankind, but is made in order to gain the secret of the knowledge of the runes. Odin's sacrifice makes him an initiate of Knowledge.

TIFERET AND INDIVIDUAL DEVELOPMENT

In terms of our individual development, Tiferet represents the transition to young adulthood. We have passed through the early stages of childhood creative activity (Hesed), when all is play and joy, into the difficulties of growing up. Gevurah is a kind of schooling where we learn first discipline imposed by others from outside and then discipline imposed from inside by our own will. We have learned what to do and what not to do. We have learned to curb our energies and enthusiasms and to channel them in order to reach goals. This is deferred gratification so beloved of middle class parenting that teaches people that in order to have good careers, they must have qualifications and in order to have good qualifications, they must study. Gevurah is about skilfully applied effort that results in outcomes. The question that must be asked at Tiferet is – what outcomes? Are the outcomes that we are directing ourselves towards really *ours*, or are they goals that have been imposed from outside by parents, teachers and society? We return here to Piero Ferrucci's book *What We May Be*. Tiferet's task for us is to discover exactly that – what we may be. Once we have goal and direction, we will then have the third aspect of what Ferrucci saw as essential in developing our will – motivation. At Tiferet we must decided what is 'me' and what is 'not me'. The great questions of life begin. 'Who am I and what am I doing here?' 'What are my goals, values and ideals?' This is the stage when we question the religious and social values of our parents. This is all part of becoming 'me'. We are leaving behind the childhood world, dominated by parents, and entering into our own 'kingdoms'.

It is important to remember that Kabbalah teaches that each of us is born with a unique role and ability to enhance the world. This is our personal contribution to the Great Work. Each one of us is a spark of the Divine, who brings light into the world by our very existence. We must find our vocation, our life's work, and dedicate ourselves to it. This is not an easy task. In previous eras parents, teachers and elders of our communities mapped out our futures for us – for good or ill. Our futures were largely determined by our gender. If we were male, certain choices were open to us. If we were female, the choices were usually few. Our vocation to be wives and mothers and this was considered a full-time career. Today this is no longer the case. Both sexes expect to live lives in which careers, relationships and parenting are important options. It may be that we decide not to pursue all three of these options, but the choices are there in a way that was not true for our predecessors. Men may choose to take a much more active role in parenting than that which was approved of for fathers and grandfathers. Women may choose to pursue a career as their first aim, rather than motherhood.

Although our choices are ours to make, they will be influenced by the extent to which we know ourselves. Unfortunately, at crucial stages when we make educational and career choices that will affect the rest of our lives, we may know ourselves little, if at all. Our parents, siblings, other relatives, friends and teachers, give us feedback on our behaviour and characteristics. We internalize these evaluations, some of which will be erroneous, and identify ourselves as a certain type of person. If we get this wrong, we may have to at some stage re-evaluate what we are doing and go back to our earlier decisions and make changes. What is important to understand is that we are more than the sum of our environmental influences. Kabbalah teaches that there is an underlying core to our personality, an individual spark that endures between incarnations. This is our True Self or the *Self*, as Jungian psychologists call it. It is the desires of the Self that are important in our life choices rather than those of the outer personality. As we approach the Tiferet stage of our lives, we begin what may be a life-long quest to find 'the real me'.

THE LIFE TASK

Tiferet is associated with the ancient myth of the dying and resurrecting God. This not only symbolizes the death and resurrection of the body, but also spiritual rebirth in our own lifetimes. The concept of an inner death and rebirth – of the old Self dying so that a new Self can be reborn from the ashes of the old – is an ancient idea found in all cultures. Tribal initiations and the initiations of the Western Mystery Tradition work on this principle. They represent stages of development when we must let go of old conditioning and patterns of thought and embrace a new and uncertain future. Change can be scary; but to move forward we must let go of whatever binds us to habits of thought, feeling and behaviour that are outworn.

Becoming what we truly are is spoken of in the Western Mystery Tradition as the Great Work. This is our life's task. The word 'work' is important here. In order to become what we are meant to be, we must find our true vocation. This means finding how we can best contribute to the world around us. It is important that we do not constantly postpone developing ourselves and expanding our horizons. How many people do you know who are always going to write that novel, move to the country, get a better job – tomorrow? Or perhaps it is when the children have grown up, when the divorce has come through, when they retire? Life is uncertain and full of change. We need to find out who we are and what we truly want *now*, for tomorrow may never come. Not exploring our talents or discovering what we can do and how best we can contribute to the greater world around us is rather like having a wardrobe full of clothes that we never wear. When we come to the end of our lives we want to feel that we have truly lived.

Of course, if we try to express ourselves, we may fail. We may find that we are not great novelists, that we hate country life, that the new job is so demanding that we yearn for the long hours of monotony that our previous job provided. Change is a risk, so is living. Without risk we are dead to life's possibilities and all it has to offer. Failure can teach us much. We learn nothing if we never try. Once we know our true vocation, we become courageous. We fight and strive in pursuit of our goal. Such conviction comes when we have found the right thing, the right way for us.

SPIRITUAL EXPERIENCE OF TIFERET

The emanation of the sefirot from Keter to Malkhut is a metaphor for the evolutionary journey of the Divine into manifestation. We, like the Divine, must evolve into our fullest manifestation or self-expression. Then, after many incarnations, we begin to evolve back to Keter, back to the Divine and reunification with Ultimate Reality. The spiritual experience of Tiferet is the Vision of the Harmony of Things. In human evolution, there are joys and sorrows. At first, in our early stages of development, these are personal.

We are focused in an egocentric view and we do not see the bigger picture. At Tiferet we realize that there is a harmony and beauty in the cycle of life, death and rebirth that is our lot and that of our fellow human beings. There is a reconciliation of pain and sorrow with pleasure and joy that can be woven into a beautiful harmonious tapestry that is our life and that of others. The Divine name in Tiferet, the Divine All-Knowing One, shows that a new perspective is gained in Tiferet. From the vantage point of the centre of the Tree, we begin to see the patterning and beauty behind this strange phenomenon, human life.

TIFERETIC QUALITIES

The Virtue or positive quality of Tiferet is known as Devotion to the Great Work. The Great Work is the transformation of humankind and this must begin with the transformation of our individual selves. In Jungian psychology, the name for this process is *individuation*. Becoming who and what we really are; the discovery of our True Will is an important goal of the mature personality. There are dangers in achieving it. This is not the be all and end all of existence but is only a stepping stone on the way to further evolution. You may have friends who have achieved some kind of spiritual breakthrough. They have been NLP'd, Rolfed, aura cleansed, initiated into the mystery, taken on by an important teacher – and they are total pains in the butt. A danger of achieving Tiferetic consciousness is that it is easy to believe that we have found the end goal; that 'this is it'. Of course, it is not; it is instead only a stage on the path. We may believe we are spiritually enlightened beings; that we have 'made it' – so why can't everyone else do it? We begin to feel that we are 'different', 'better', 'special'. Of course we are special; but so is everyone else in her or his own way. The 'vice' or negative quality of Tiferet is pride and an aspect of pride is mistaking the part for the whole. Many people on the way to enlightenment make this mistake. They achieve a spiritual breakthrough. Perhaps others recognize their 'star' qualities and come to them for teaching. They begin to know pride and in knowing pride create a barrier between themselves and the true source of their being. Here we return to the need for one of the positive qualities of Hesed – laughter. In our spiritual evolution, a healthy dose of Gevuric cynicism can also be helpful from time to time.

EXPLORING TIFERET

The Western Mystery Tradition has created various symbol systems that are designed to trigger effects in the human psyche. The pathways between the different sefirot, for instance, have been 'pathworked' or visualized in meditative process by thousands of people over hundreds of years. Such spiritual work leaves traces in the human collective unconscious. If we use the right processes of visualization, we can tap into the pathways to the sefirot and into magical images associated with the sefirot. The Western Mystery Tradition has worked over many years with building visualized Temples for each of the sefirot. These Temples are not physical buildings but are states of consciousness triggered by the use of the shared symbol system of the Western Mystery Tradition.

EXERCISE 1: TEMPLE OF TIFERET

Below is an active imagination exercise to help you get in touch the Divine in Tiferet by contacting the Temple of Tiferet. First you will need to make a drawing of the Temple of Tiferet. Take a large piece of paper and draw a diagram or sketch using coloured pens or paints of approximately the right colour. If you are not an artist you may find it easier to draw the temple as a plan, imagining that you are standing above the room.

1. The Temple is a square room with golden-yellow walls.
2. Opposite the door is an enormous stained-glass window. Its colours are yellow, gold, rose, red and orange. Sunlight is streaming through, making patterns of coloured light on the floor. You may see a picture in the stained glass, or perhaps a pattern.
3. In the centre of the room is a square-topped altar covered with a gold cloth.
4. On the altar are two candlesticks with lighted yellow candles. Between the candlesticks is a golden vase containing six bright yellow flowers.

In front of the vase of flowers is an incense burner. Sweet-smelling incense smoke rises into the temple.

5. Behind the altar and in front of the stained-glass window is a high-backed wooden chair.
6. Inside the Temple, it is as warm as a summer's day.

Once you have made your drawing or painting, learn to visualize it so that you can imagine it without looking at the drawing. To practise, visualize the Temple one stage at a time: first the room, then the altar and then the objects on the altar. Now try to hold a complete image of the Temple in your mind. Practise visualizing the Tiferet Temple for a few days, until you can visualize it well.

THE DIVINE IN TIFERET

Once you can visualize the Temple, go on to the next stage – a visualization of an image of deity in Tiferet. A simple way of doing this is to visualize the Divine in Tiferet as a Solar King. One of Tiferet's titles is *Melekh*, King, and Tiferet is associated with the Sun. The idea of a solar deity is found in many spiritual traditions. In Irish mythology, we have Lugh the Light bearer. In Norse tradition, we have Baldur the Beautiful. In Egypt, the Sun God was Ra. In Greece, we have Helios and Apollo. In Christian tradition, there is the image of Christ the risen King.

1. Visualize the Temple of Tiferet as before.
2. The Temple is warm and sweetly smelling. You feel a great sense of peace and relaxation. Bright sunlight streams through the stained-glass window.
3. The light through the window becomes brighter and brighter. Golden light begins to form a column on the floor behind the altar in front of the high-backed chair.
4. The golden light begins to take the shape of a tall man with long flowing hair. You sense a presence of great power, gentleness and love.
5. The figure becomes solid, three-dimensional. An image of the Solar King has appeared. Commune with him for a while. Perhaps he has something to tell you, or to give you.
6. When you feel the time is right, bid him farewell and let his presence fade.

7. Afterwards make some notes. Describe the Solar King's appearance, your feelings and sensations, and any message or gift he had for you. You could draw or paint an image of the Solar King.

EXERCISE 2: THE DIVINE FEMININE IN TIFERET

In order to evolve your idea of Tiferet further, you might like to experiment with visualizing the Divine in Tiferet not as Solar King, but as Solar Queen. Here is an exercise where we think of the solar force of Tiferet as female.

1. Create the temple visualization.
2. The temple is warm and sweetly smelling. You feel a great sense of peace.
3. Bright sunlight is streaming through the stained-glass window.
4. You feel yourself relaxing and becoming drowsy.
5. The light through the window is becoming brighter and brighter. It seems as though the light is pouring down in a golden glow onto the high-backed chair behind the altar.
6. The golden light seems to be forming into a shape seated on the high-backed chair.
7. You sense a presence of great power and love.
8. You see the silhouette of a majestic woman with long flowing hair.
9. The shape becomes solid, three-dimensional. The Solar Goddess has appeared. Commune with her for a while. Perhaps she has something to tell you or to give you.
10. When you feel the time is right, bid her farewell and let her presence fade.
11. Afterwards write up your notes. Describe how the Goddess appeared to you, the feelings and sensations you had, and any message or gift she had for you. How did your experience of the Solar Queen compare with that of the Solar King? What differences did you notice in the energy, feeling, tone, or insights of the two experiences? What can this tell you?

EXERCISE 3: BRINGING HARMONY INTO YOUR LIFE

We can bring the energy of a sefirah into our lives by endeavouring to develop the qualities of the sefirah within ourselves. We can help ourselves to do this by creating the right ambience in our homes. Our unconscious minds are highly influenced by our surroundings and by symbol and colour. This is one of the reasons why many religious traditions make use of signs, symbols, chants, mantras and visual imagery in their temples and religious ceremonies. One way of helping bring Tiferetic influence into your life is to make a Tiferetic altar or shrine as a focus for its energy. Find a small table or shelf that you can fill with Tiferetic symbolism. Cover this with a yellow or gold cloth. Place gold-coloured candlesticks on it with gold-coloured candles. Place fresh golden flowers on it in a gold-coloured vase. You can also use touches of rose pink – perhaps in your flowers. Rose pink is a colour in the Western Mystery Tradition associated with the Divine energy of the sefirah of Tiferet. Burn some incense daily on your altar or use perfumed candles. Take a few moments each day to light your candles and/or incense and to meditate on golden light.

Also at this point, you can meditate on bringing the healing energy of Tiferet into your body. The Kabbalistic Cross is a self-blessing exercise drawn from the Western Mystery Tradition. It is particularly helpful to do each day on waking. It is a protective rite that can be used to banish unwanted influences from our homes and lives in order to leave a clear space in the psyche where new energy can manifest. You could do the exercise in your office, before other staff arrive. It can be used as a concentration exercise and it can be done by visualization if you find office Kabbalah a bit inconvenient.

This blessing invokes the protection of the Divine and of powerful angels. The best-known version is that created by the magical order the Golden Dawn, which had many powerful women magicians. The exercise is based on Jewish prayers but uses different attributions of angels to directions than Jewish tradition. Angels are mighty powers within the universe that order creation and take a positive interest in humankind. Like us they are conscious beings, but they do not have bodily form. The winged images with which they are depicted in painting are human images designed to help us understand their nature. In early Jewish texts only three angels are mentioned. Their names are based on the Hebrew Divine name in Hesed – El. They are Mikael or *Mi KaEl* 'He who is like El', Gabriel or Gavri El 'Strength of El', and Uriel 'Fire of El'. The Kabbalistic Cross introduces a fourth angel – Rafael 'Healing of El'.

THE KABBALISTIC CROSS

1. Stand facing East, the direction of the rising Sun, and the direction of Tiferet.
2. With your hands at chest height, face your palms forwards towards the East and say, 'Before me Rafael.' Now turn your hands so that your palms face behind you and say, 'Behind me Gavriel.'
3. Lower your left arm and turn your right palm outwards. Say, 'To my right hand Mikael.' Now lower your right arm and turn your left palm outwards and say, 'To my left hand Uriel.'
4. Using both hands, form a triangle with the fingers of each hand pointing upwards and the thumbs horizontal and touching one another.

The position of the hands when beginning the Kabbalistic Cross

5. Raise your hands in their triangle in front of your forehead and say: 'Atah' (Thou art). Visualize a column of white light above your head, pouring down on you and bathing you in light.

6. Move your hands down to crotch level, turn the triangle of your hands upside down so your fingers point to the ground and say, 'Malkhut' (the Kingdom).

7. Turn the triangle upwards and raise your hands to the level of your right shoulder. Say, 'Ve Gevurah' (Power).

8. Move your hands across at shoulder height to your left shoulder and say, 'Ve Gedulah' (Love).

9. Open your hands at chest height and stand with palms outwards to greet the universe and say, 'Le olam' (for eternity).

10. Then say if you wish, 'Amen' or 'So mote it be'.

11. Visualize Divine golden energy pouring into the crown of your head. Visualize this energy filling your skull and your neck. It flows into your shoulders, arms and hands. It flows down through your trunk, soothing the vital organs within and giving them healing. Visualize golden light flowing down into your sexual organs and then down through your thighs, knees and feet. Do this exercise six times, until you feel the healing golden light energizing your body. Now say:

Divine One, Bringer of healing energy and light,
allow Thy power and energy to flow through me,
energize me throughout my day
and keep me close to the source of your radiant being.
Amen, [or So mote it be].

12. Visualize the flow of golden energy ceasing to enter your crown, rather like a tap being turned off. You are now replenished with energy and ready to face the world.

TO NETZAH

Tiferet is the point of balance. At Netzah, which follows, we draw closer to the human realm. Let us enter the realm of feeling, and the realm of human love.

Tiferet – Beauty, Harmony

Titles: Melekh – King, Rahamin – compassion or charity, Zoar Anpin – Lesser Countenance or Impatient One
Images: Child, monarch, sacrificed God

Divine aspect

Hebrew Divine Name: *Jehovah Eloah va Daat* – Divine All-Knowing One
Deities in other traditions: Tammuz (Babylonian sacrificial God), Odin (King of Norse Gods), Lugh (Celtic light-bearer God), Rhiannon (Welsh solar Goddess), Grania (Irish solar Goddess), Christ (the King), Isis (saviour Goddess), Sekmet (healer Goddess), Helios (Greek), Apollo (Greek), Ra (Egyptian), Baldur (Norse).
Spiritual Paths: Initiatory mystery traditions

Correspondences in the Physical universe

In the Cosmos: Shemesh – the Sun
Number: 6
Colour: Yellow

Correspondences in Humankind

Spiritual Experience: Vision of Harmony
Positive quality: Devotion to the Great Work
Negative quality: Pride
In the human body: Trunk

Notes

1. Variously translated as 'Transcendental Influx Consciousness' and 'Intelligence of Mediating Influence'.
2. 'Healing Hands: The Birth of the NFSH Rose' *Healing Today, Journal of the National Federation of Spiritual Healers*, No 76, summer 1995 (page 5).
3. Kaplan (1989, page 72).

7

NETZAH – VICTORY OR ENDURANCE

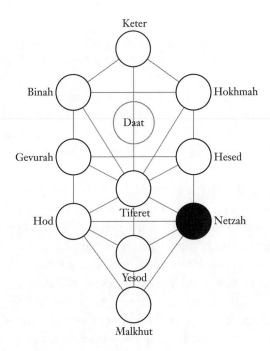

The seventh path is called 'Hidden Consciousness' (Sekhel Nistar),
because it is the radiance that illuminates the spiritual powers
that are seen by inner contemplation and by the ecstasy of Faith.
SEFER YETZIRAH

Tiferet, the sefirah of beauty, emanates the sefirah of Netzah, Victory or Endurance. In Netzah the Divine conceives the urge to create more complex forms in matter. At Tiferet, the Divine may pause and look backwards to Its own source and origin and forwards to where it might go and what it might become. After Tiferet, there is a fragmentation – that which was a unified whole becomes separate and individual. In evolutionary terms, we have the emergence of the main species groups. During the course of evolution many life forms emerge, but many do not stand the test of Netzah. They do not endure. From the development of eukaryotic cells that can process energy from sunlight, we have the beginning in Netzah of the diversity of biological life as we know it. In the course of evolution, some eukaryotic cells combined to form multi-celled organisms and began to diversify dramatically. We now have five species groups: animals, fungi, green plants, red algae and a more recently discovered group called stramenopiles, most of which look like plants but do not photosynthesize. While we are most aware of the higher forms of biological life such as plants, animals and ourselves, it is important to remember that these evolved forms of life are a minority on our planet. Microbes are still the most prolific species and compared to them, higher life forms such as ourselves are merely evolutionary afterthoughts.

If we think of the Divine as energy, it is as though at Netzah separate energy sparks have broken away to seek their own destiny. There may be a deeply buried memory of their Divine origin, but on a conscious level at Netzah each aspect of creation becomes separated from other aspects of creation. We have the beginning in Netzah of the beautiful diversity of the natural world. Creation involves desire, just as creation of a child springs from desire. It is this desire that ascetic paths would have us renounce. Netzah is associated with Venus, the planet of physical love, desire and sexuality. Netzah is about combination and joining – in many possible different ways. Recent research by scientist Peter Wirtz of the Max Planck Institute in Germany shows that one important way in which new species arise is through cross-species mating. Females of one species seek out males from another species rather than their own. This usually happens when, through some natural disaster, males of their own species are difficult to find. The sexual instinct is so strong that other compatible males are sought. From these unions, new hybrid species arise; thus manifests the diversity that is at the heart of Netzah.

NETZAH AND NATURE

Netzah's predominant colour in the Western Mystery Tradition is green, the colour of Nature. Netzah is related particularly to plant life, which is the necessary precursor for animal and human life. Once plants began to give off oxygen in photosynthesis, they produced an oxygen-rich atmosphere that enabled oxygen-breathing creatures like humans to evolve.

Netzah's connection with the world of Nature means that in the Western Mystery Tradition, there is a strong link with the mythical and magical Otherworld that is populated by devas or fairies; beings that are conscious but do not have the same physical bodies as ourselves. The idea that we share our natural world with other beings who live a parallel existence to ourselves and are sometimes visible and sometimes not is a very old one found all over the world. Perhaps it was our ancestors' over-active imagination on dark winter nights that populated the Otherworld with mysterious beings of great beauty. Perhaps it is an expression of a reality that we do not understand. Whatever the truth, there are many myths and legends which speak of beings of the Otherworld. In the West, its inhabitants were known as the fairy folk. Many are the tales of those who went to dwell for a while in the land of fairy, or *Tir na N'Og*, the Land of Youth as it is in the Irish. Tir na N'Og got its name because those who dwell there are ever young. It was said to be the dwelling place of the dead between incarnations. It also operates under different time-space principles from our everyday world.

THE DIVINE IN NETZAH

The Hebrew Divine name in Netzah is *Jehovah Tzevaot*, God of Hosts. Here we have a sense of the One becoming the many, the unicellular become the complex multicellular. In the Western Mystery Tradition, the Netzahian current is found in those deities most associated with sexual love. In the Roman pantheon we have the Goddess Venus and in ancient Greece, Aphrodite. Both had sons – Venus had Cupid and Aphrodite had Eros – who helped them with their work. From Eros comes our word 'erotic'. Erotic energy is the essence of Netzah. From Cupid we have the image of Cupid's arrow that strikes us when we least expect it and leads to a desire that cannot be quenched except through sexual love. The planet Venus from which the Roman Goddess takes her name is *Nogah* in Hebrew. Nogah means glow, twilight. It is associated with Venus as the Evening Star and represents the vagina.

NETZAH AND SEXUALITY

The celebration of the erotic as Divine is at the heart of the mystery of Netzah. The Netzahian current manifests in many spiritual traditions. The most obvious spiritual paths outside Judaism are those associated with sexuality, such as Tantra in Eastern traditions and, in the West, some of the inner mysteries of Wicca. In Hinduism, for instance, carvings of men and women in sexual union appear on the walls of temples and the lingam or penis of the God Shiva is venerated as a symbol of sublime holiness. Tantra recognizes the existence of a mysterious psycho-physical energy called *kundalini*. This can be harnessed to cause spiritual transformation. The lesson of Netzah is that harmonious spiritual integration may be best achieved through sensory experience and everyday life. Spirituality has tended to take us away from the body, something that has negative consequences for women. Fortunately, Kabbalah does not advocate this type of practice. The requirement that men who studied Kabbalah must be married and not young meant that male students of mysticism could experience sexuality in its fullness and could continue to do so, though only with their wives. Indeed a happy married life was seen as a firm basis from which to proceed to explore the heights of mysticism rather than a distraction from it.

In Netzah, we see that the human body, with all its biological and psychological processes, is an instrument through which cosmic forces operate. Human sexuality is therefore a reflection of the interaction of force and form within the cosmic Tree of Life. The union of the Divine Male (God) and Divine Female (Goddess or Shekhinah) as symbolized by the union of their worshippers transports the worshippers to supreme heights of spiritual ecstasy. Through this union, worshippers can achieve a state of unity of consciousness between self and other which is a reflection of the unity of consciousness of the Divine Oneness in Keter. Having experienced this temporarily, it is as though we have a map within our psyches to help us find that ultimate destination once again. We have been transported there by almost magical means and now we must go the hard and long way, by foot as it were, but knowing that the destination exists and that we can get there. The task of our incarnations is to reach this state of union permanently. In Netzah, the sex drive, or what Freud calls libido, is seen as but an aspect of the spirit's longing for perfection and reunion with the Divine.

THE SONG OF SONGS

The best-known piece of Jewish erotic poetry is the *Shir ha-Shirim*, or 'Songs of Songs' from the Bible. The 'Song of Songs' is highly regarded amongst Kabbalists. In the *Bahir* there is a dialogue that concludes: 'All Scripture is holy, and all the Torah is holy but the 'Song of Songs' is Holy of Holies.'[1] Kabbalists recommend meditating upon the 'Song of Songs' as a sacred act to help us commune with the Divine. What is surprising about the 'Songs of Songs' is that, unlike most Biblical text, much of it is spoken by a female voice. In the 'Song of Songs', Judaism begins to sound remarkably like Tantra. Here are some extracts.

Lady:
Let him kiss me with the kisses of his mouth –
for your love is more delightful than wine.
Pleasing is the fragrance of your perfumes;
your name is like perfume poured out.
No wonder the maidens love you!
Take me away with you – let us hurry!
Let the king bring me into his chambers –
we rejoice and delight in you,
we will praise your love more than wine.
How right they are to adore you!

May the wine go straight to my lover,
flowing gently over his lips and teeth.
I belong to my lover, and his desire is for me.
Come, my lover, let us go to the countryside,
let us spend the night in the villages.
Let us go early to the vineyards
to see if the vines have budded,
If their blossoms have opened,
and, if the pomegranates are in bloom,
there I will give you my love.
The mandrakes send out their fragrance,
and at our door is every delicacy, both new and old,
that I have stored up for you, my lover.[2]

Here we recognize how an erotic passion can transport those possessed by it into such heights of ecstasy that it seems a true experience of the Divine. The 'Song of Songs' also speaks with the voice of the Lover.

Lover:
Arise, my darling, my beautiful one, and come with me.
See – the winter is past;
the rains are over and gone;
flowers appear on the earth;
the season of singing has come,
the cooing of doves is heard in our land,
the fig tree forms its early fruit,
the blossoming vines spread their fragrance.
Arise, come, my darling;
my beautiful one, come with me.

My dove, in the clefts of the rock,
in the hiding places on the mountainside,
show me your face, let me hear your voice;
for your voice is sweet, and your face is lovely.[3]

This is the loving eroticism of Netzah. Kabbalah sanctifies sexuality so that a union between woman and man is seen as a reflection of the union between the female and male aspects of the Divine. This can be the union of Binah, the Supernal Mother, with Hokhmah, the Supernal Father, or the union between the bride and Divine Daughter, Malkhut, with the bridegroom and Divine Son, Tiferet. The covenant of circumcision can be seen to represent a sanctifying by the Divine of the emotions and desires associated with sex. Sex is seen as a human being's opportunity to regain wholeness. Sexuality becomes a path to spirituality.

Certain sexual techniques are taught in Kabbalah, as in Tantra, to prolong sexual union in order to transcend physical pleasure and to enter into a state of spiritual ecstasy. One technique involves focusing on the ten toes, each one representing a sefirah. The toes on the right foot represent, from the big toe outwards, the 'masculine' sefirot of Keter, Hokhmah, Hesed, Tiferet, and Netzah. The toes on the left foot, from the big toe outwards, represent Binah, Gevurah, Hod, Yesod and Malkhut. Focusing on the toes one by one, from the Keter toe down to Malkhut, helps concentrate spiritual energy into the penis and vagina, both to give greater sexual control and to ensure healthy children.

Kabbalists celebrated sexuality on the night of the Sabbath. Pious scholars were taught that on other nights of the week, they should restrain from sex and devote their energies to studying the Torah. On the seventh night, it was time to welcome the Sabbath Queen and Bride. The Kabbalists of 16th-century Safed included in their Sabbath celebration a poem in Aramaic written by Kabbalistic sage Isaac Luria. This described the union of Tiferet with Malkhut.

Let me sing praises of him who enters the gates
of the orchard of apple trees, holy are they!

Let us invite her now, with a freshly set table,
with a goodly lamp which sheds light on our heads.

Right and left, and the Bride in between
comes forth in her jewels and sumptuous garments.

Her husband embraces her and, with her Yesod –
which gives her pleasure, he presses her mightily.

Cries and sighs have stopped and ceased,
new faces come, spirits and souls.

He brings her great joy in a double measure,
light pours upon her, and blessings on end.[4]

Here Yesod represents the penis which becomes "hers" during the sexual act. Sexual relations were to take place ideally after midnight on the Sabbath as this was the holiest hour, after the husband had recited the formula:

I fulfil the commandment of sexual relations for the unification of the Holy One, Blessed Be He, and the Shekhinah.[5]

If the couple performed their union at this time, they would be imitating the sacred marriage of the male and female aspects of the Divine. Kabbalists were encouraged to sanctify sexuality and to see it as a holy act.

No other moment is like the ecstasy of the moment
when spirit cleaves to spirit in a kiss.
ZOHAR 2:146A

Sex is sanctified in Judaism in a way that it is not in Christianity. Sex in mystical literature, Jewish and otherwise, is also a metaphor for other forms of union, such as that between the human and the Divine. It is striking how often the link between the mystical seeker and the Divine is expressed in terms of a *hieros gamos* or sacred marriage. In the Christian monastic tradition, for instance, the nun is spoken of as being married to Christ her Divine bridegroom. Traditionally, she came to profess her vows in a bridal gown.

TITLES AND IMAGES

Netzah translates as 'Victory' or 'Endurance' and is described as a pouring out of 'brilliant splendour'. Netzah means Victory, but Victory over what? Victory requires something to conquer or a battle to win. In Netzah we have the triumph of the possible. The Divine is doing something extraordinary. It is bestowing consciousness on material creatures. It will make humankind as Gods. 'Victory' and 'brilliant' are words that arouse our emotions. The Netzahian world is a world of emotional drives. 'Emotional' can have negative connotations, but it is important to remember that our emotions and passions are driving forces behind great artistic and cultural movements, and also movements such as social reform. We become emotionally engaged and this arouses the energy to make and to do.

The image of Netzah is of a beautiful woman. Here we return once more to the sexual mysteries that turn eroticism into union with the Divine. One of the primary human emotions is sexual love. Jungian psychology talks about four types of archetypal male image – the spiritual teacher (Hesed), the king (Tiferet), the lover and hero (Netzah) and the man of animalistic passions and physical strength (Yesod). In Netzah, we have the perfect knight of courtly love and of the Troubadour tradition that flourished at the same time and place as Kabbalah's flowering in 12th-century Provence. Classic Netzahian heroes are Lancelot, who risks all for his love of his Queen Guinevere, and Shakespeare's hero Romeo with his doomed love for Juliet.

The association of Shakespeare with Netzah is apt, because Netzah is the sefirah of artists of sound, word and image – musicians, poets and artists. It is no coincidence that artists often transgress the sexual boundaries of their societies. Creativity and sexuality can feed one another – two dynamic forces seeking to express the energy of Netzah. Netzah harnesses the creative outpouring of Hesed above it into artistic endeavour; although the technical skills that underpin artistic creativity are the province of the mind (Hod) and physical skill (Malkhut).

The outpouring of love that is Hesed is received into Netzah unmediated by Tiferet's balancing mechanisms. The result is excess; another problem frequently faced by the creative amongst us. Netzah can be the archetypal hippie paradise where love and peace prevail, flowers are passed around, together with various intoxicating and somewhat addictive substances, and life is focused on pleasure and enjoyment. This is the Irish land of Tir na N'Og, the Land of the ever young, and of all those who would be ever young. The world of rock music is fed by Netzah, as are all of the arts that worship the 'beautiful people'. Beverley Hills is a Netzahian paradise, with its magnificent gardens, houses and pools, and all the luxury and unhappiness that luxury unchecked can bring.

NETZAH AND INDIVIDUAL DEVELOPMENT

In terms of our development, Netzah corresponds to the stage when we form love relationships. It is when we enter the romantic world. We experience the intense, joyous and dreadful pangs of first love – which usually ends disastrously. Everything is emotionally intensified so that we cannot imagine living without the object of our passion. We are back to the doomed love of Romeo and Juliet. Netzah's dreams are focused on the needs of the individual and not of society. They are the stuff of the heart and not of the head. Often they cannot withstand the harsh tests of reality. These may also be relationships that express Netzah's vice or negative quality – selfishness, which is subjectivity taken too far. This is the besetting sin of those who become totally immersed in their relationships or creative vision to the exclusion of other obligations. We become centred on our own objectives and nothing else matters to us. Other obligations are forgotten.

NETZAHIAN QUALITIES

If we are lucky, our early relationships give way to the joy of a true relationship with a partner with whom we can share our lives. This is when we must learn the positive quality of Netzah, which is unselfishness. Without this, relationships are doomed to failure. Unselfishness is a state of consciousness where we treat others with love and respect. Another word we could use is 'inclusiveness'. We see ourselves as part of the great tapestry of life, with a sense of connectedness to those around us. This is an advanced state of consciousness and not easy to attain all the time. We have glimpses of it, but often we retreat into our own needs. Instead of sharing and participating, we take and demand. We fall victim to the negative quality or vice of Netzah – selfishness or lust.

Netzah takes us into the realm of feeling. Of course, feelings can be dangerous. We cannot follow our feelings indiscriminately. Often we can be swayed by irrational and negative feelings and emotions. The colour of Netzah is green in the Western Mystery Tradition, a colour often associated with envy. This is the negative feeling that makes us compare our lot with others. It convinces us that our possessions, relationships, physical appearance, job, material prospects or whatever, are worse than those of others. Instead of aspiring to evolve and develop our own qualities, we desire those of others and make ourselves miserable.

SPIRITUAL EXPERIENCE OF NETZAH

The spiritual experience of Netzah is the Vision of Beauty Triumphant. Think of the image of a woman going to meet her chosen lover, radiant with the knowledge that she is loved totally and without reservation. This is Netzah. Think of the image of a young couple wrapped in one another's arms, or of an elderly couple whose touch can still make each other's pulses throb, eyes glow and juices run. Think of the hymns to loving sexuality that appear in the 'Song of Songs' and in the *Rubaiyat of Omar Khayyam*. These are images of Netzah and speak of the experience of Beauty Triumphant.

Beauty is not something frivolous or 'the icing on the cake'. The human spirit craves beauty like the body craves food. Beauty can sustain our spirits as food does our bodies. Beauty can precipitate for us what the psychologist Abraham Maslow called 'peak experiences'. Dr. Viktor Frankl wrote of his experiences in a concentration camp and of how even in the darkest time of desperation, the beauties of nature could transfix the prisoners, liberating their spirits for a brief but sustaining moment from the terror and horror that surrounded them. He recalled, when on a train from Auschwitz to a Bavarian camp, how he and his companions were mesmerized by the sight through the barred windows of the railway carriage of a beautiful sunset over the mountains of Salzburg.[6] In Nature's beauty we see the victorious triumph of Netzah, the Divine expressing Itself in the perfection and beauty of matter.

We also find the Vision of Beauty Triumphant in great artistic creations. The human artist becomes the Divine Creator/Creatrix and changes matter into new and beauteous forms. Great figures from the twentieth century spring to mind like the opera singer Maria Callas and the dancer Rudolf Nureyev. To hear Callas or to see Nureyev was a spiritual as well as an artistic experience. Music is connected with Hod, but to interpret music in more than a technical way requires the participation of the passion and energy of Netzah. Similarly, dance is partly an athletic activity and sport connected with Yesod and Malkhut; but to raise dance to an art form requires the aesthetic appreciation of Netzah, as well as a huge dose of the disciplined study and precision of Hod. A difference between the dancer and the athlete is that for a dancer physical perfection is used for artistic interpretation and communicating understanding of human life. In the athlete, the body is used to express the perfection of the body and competitive striving.

EXPLORING NETZAH

EXERCISE 1: ACCEPTING YOUR SENSUALITY

Netzah is related to sexuality, but for many people sexuality is not a positive experience. It is easy for children and adolescents to absorb negative messages about their bodies and sexuality. Sexuality becomes something shameful and forbidden rather than spontaneous and free. Of course, in our HIV age, we cannot return to a Garden of Eden of sexual freedom and abandon. Sexuality today must be accompanied by responsible awareness, but sexuality is still one of the great pleasures and joys of human existence, which can arouse us to new visions and to personal joy. If we are to experience the joy of Netzah, we must first come to terms with our own Netzahian selves, our erotic selves. This is an exercise to help you contact your early guilt-free self.

1. For this exercise, you need quiet, privacy, warmth and soft lighting. You may want to light a candle and to burn some perfumed oil. The exercise is best done lying down. You could write or type the exercise in large print so that you can refer to the instructions as you go along. Alternatively, you could read the instructions onto a cassette so you can play them back. In this case, leave gaps for visualization between each instruction.

2. Relax and allow tension in your body to seep away.

3. Now imagine that you are swimming in a warm clear blue sea. Above you, the sun shines in a cloudless blue sky. You are naked and the water caresses your body as you swim through the warm sea.

4. You are swimming towards a silvery white sandy shore. The water becomes shallow and you stand up and wade onto the shore. There are no other footprints here. You are alone and there is nothing to fear.

5. Beneath your bare feet you feel the hot sand. A gentle breeze caresses your body and the warm sun dries your skin.

6. Beyond the shore, the sand gives way to lush green trees covered in fruit. Through the trees is a sandy path. You follow the path. Gradually the sand gives way to soft green grass. You feel a soft carpet of cool greenness beneath your feet.

7. You find yourself approaching a temple with yellow sandstone walls. A sweet smell of incense wafts out through the open doors.

8. You enter the temple, naked and unafraid. In the centre of the temple is an altar on which burns a vigil fire. A green altar cloth with embroidered flowers, trees and birds covers the altar. On the wall behind the altar is a stained-glass window with a beautiful face in the centre like that of an angel with flaming red hair. All is light, warm and joyful.

9. You stand in front of the altar and commune with the vigil fire. The flames leap higher as though to greet you. A vision appears in the flames of the interior of another temple in a warm country long ago. There white-robed priestesses and priests came to tend the temple fire, but here there is only you. You are sad that so few come to tend

the flame; for you sense that within each of us we have need of this vigil fire.

10. And then you sense in the temple the presence of the Divine. You stand before the Divine naked and unashamed. Divine love flows over you, bathing your body in golden light, loving all of you – body, soul, mind and spirit. You are a vessel of the Divine Spirit that watches over all. You sense that there is no shame in loving desire and no shame in the sexual love of another; for all love is a reflection of the love that the Divine has for us. You commune with this feeling for a while – a feeling of total acceptance of all that you are – beneath the loving gaze of the Divine Father and Mother of all.

11. When you are ready you depart. You follow the grassy path back through the trees. The grass gives way to sand and you emerge on the sandy beach. You wade into the blue sea and when it is deep enough you begin to swim. You turn on your back and float in the warm and welcoming sea. You float until you find yourself dreaming once more of your everyday room in your everyday world. You sense it is time to return.

12. You open your eyes and you are back in your room once more. You are alone, at peace, and with a memory of love and acceptance for your body and yourself.

EXERCISE 2: BRINGING NETZAH INTO YOUR LIFE

Netzah's astrological planet is Venus. Venus relates to love, beauty and sensuality. Here are some things that you can do to develop your Netzahian qualities:

1. Look at your home. Are there ways you could bring more beauty into it? Bringing beauty into your home need not mean spending lots of money. Plants, flowers and aromatic oils are inexpensive ways of making your home more beautiful both visually and aromatically. What about sound? What music do you find beautiful and do you take enough time to play and enjoy it? Play music more and watch the television less.

2. Look at what you wear and the colours that you wear. Do you wear colour – or are you colourless? Do you know which colours suit you? Have you ever had a colour consultation? Many people go through life wearing colours that do not suit their skin tone at all. Colour is not just for women. Male politicians and other men in the public eye go to great lengths to ensure that they use colour to enhance their appearance and image. If you do not know your own personal colour palette consider going for a session with a colour consultant. You can find addresses in lifestyle and women's magazines.
3. Netzah is associated in the Western Mystery Tradition with the element of Fire. Netzah burns, not with the uncontrolled energy of Gevurah, but with the warmth of a summer's day. Netzahian energy is the feeling we have after a long lazy summer afternoon when heat has relaxed the muscles of our bodies and freed us of all tension; when we feel totally in harmony with the physical and animal aspect of ourselves.
4. If you want to bring Netzahian energy into your life, make a small shrine or altar in your home dedicated to this aspect of the Divine. On your altar or shrine, place items with Netzahian associations, such as ornaments made of green glass, a statue of a beautiful Goddess, roses or an oil burner to burn aromatic oils.

These simple actions on the physical plane will draw the energy of Netzah into your life. When your life contains Netzahian energy, you will draw in more Netzahian energy – like attracts like. If you want to attract love, you must create a loving environment and understand that the universe loves you. You are a child of the Divine.

EXERCISE 3: MYSELF AS LOVER AND FRIEND

It is easy for us to feel sexual love towards another person and equally easy for us to experience all the jealousy and possessiveness that are the negative qualities of that emotion. What is not so easy is the art of being a good lover and friend to our sexual partners. This is an exercise to help you explore how you relate to others as lover and friend.

1. Take five pieces of paper and a pen to write. Think for a while about the history of your sexual relationships. Who were the three most significant lovers in your life? 'Significant' can include significantly good lovers and significantly bad ones.

2. Write the names of your three most significant lovers on three separate pieces of paper.

3. Answer these questions for each relationship in turn. It is probably easiest to deal with the relationships in chronological order, from the earliest to most recent.
   - How did you meet – where, when, in what circumstances?
   - Was it by chance, through a friend, through work, through social activities?
   - What were the advantages and disadvantages of meeting in the way that you did?
   - How long did the relationship last?
   - How did you feel when it ended – if it has?

4. Now answer:
   - What were the good things about your partner and about the relationship?
   - How did you behave in the relationship – what did you give, what did you take, what did you like about the way you behaved, what did you dislike?
   - What were the bad things about your partner and about the relationship?
   - Once you have covered all three relationships, consider the three together:
   - What did you learn from these relationships – about yourself, about others, and about relationships in general?

5. Now take the fourth piece of paper and write down the name or names of up to three people whom you might have liked to have a relationship with but did not. For each one, write down why you did not pursue the relationship. Was it because it was impractical – circumstances kept you apart, or perhaps he or she was already committed to someone else? Was it because you did not show that you were interested? If not, why not? Did you rate yourself as likely to fail, or unable to meet the other person's standards?

6. Now look at all the relationships that you have had and that you would have liked to have had:
   - What are the common features that you found – good and bad?
   - Think about your current relationship or the next relationship you would like to have. Are there any negative feelings that hold you back from having the type of relationships you would like? Can you recognize these feelings in the relationships that you have had before or would have liked to have had, but did not?
7. Now take a fifth piece of paper and write down all the positive qualities that you have to offer to someone as a friend and lover. Also write down things that you might like to change about yourself to be a better friend and lover.

You have now thought about relationships and about how you behave within relationships. You may have seen patterns that you tend to repeat. Some of these patterns may be positive, but some of them may be just the opposite – negative patterns that you would like to change. Remember that loving is an art and skill. If you have not experienced positive relationships in your life and have not observed other members of your family in positive relationships, then you may need to learn how to make successful interactions with others. If this is the case, here are some ideas to help you.

Spontaneity and *playfulness* are important in sexual love. In your relationships, do you make the first move, or must your partner always approach you? Do you do sensual activities for fun, like massage, taking a bath or shower together, going away for a weekend and spending a long time together in bed? Do you show that you care? Do you tell your partner that you love him or her? Do you buy him or her surprise presents – and remember the occasions when you should buy a present! Touching, telling and showing are all ways of demonstrating our Netzahian feelings for one another.

Touch gives us the reassurance that our bodies are acceptable to others. Touch returns us to the world of childhood when our baby bodies are loved by our parents as a miracle of incarnation. Touch restores us to the Garden of Eden when all is beauteous balance. We return to a world of lost innocence. Images of Hod are frequently associated with the purifying and testing processes of the desert. We are expelled from the Eden world of childhood into the rigours of adult life. Netzahian sensual experience can return us for a brief time to that Eden world; not to escape, but to fortify ourselves for the reality outside. A truly loving sexual relationship can bring the joy of being loved and accepted in our entirety. This is the great gift of Netzah.

Sound, in the form of words of love, gives us a different message from that of touch. Words speak to the conscious mind and to our self-awareness. The words 'I love you' are a miracle when they are spoken in sincerity by one human being to another, to express our reverence and devotion to another of our species in whom we recognize the Divine indwelling spirit that we both share. What can compare to the feeling that such words arouse; especially when they are accompanied by touch?

Gestures in the form of the daily acts that surround a loving relationship, such as the unexpected cup of coffee or tea brought when we obviously need it but have not asked, the bath run when we return exhausted from a long working day, a spontaneous gift – these are all Netzahian in that they come from a movement of giving, the movement that is the keynote of the Pillar of Force. When we love, we give. This is the secret of love. Try it.

TO HOD

From Netzah we cross to the world of the mind and the pillar of Form. We cross to Hod.

Netzah – Victory

Titles: Firmness, Valour, Endurance
Image: A beautiful naked woman

Divine Aspect

Hebrew Divine Name: *Jehovah Tzevaot* – God of Hosts
Deities in other traditions: Venus (Roman Goddess), Aphrodite (Greek Goddess), Eros (Son of Venus), Cupid (Son of Aphrodite), Freya and Frey (Norse Vanir Goddess and God of love and fertility)
Spiritual Paths: Tantra, Wicca, some aspects of Kabbalah

Correspondences in the Physical Universe

In the Cosmos: Nogah – Venus
Number: 7
Colour: Emerald green

Correspondences in Humankind

Spiritual experience: Vision of beauty triumphant
Positive quality: Unselfishness (inclusiveness)
Negative quality: Lust (selfishness)
In the human body: Left hip and leg, the vagina

Notes

1. Kaplan (1989, page 180).
2. Song of Songs 1:2–4 and 7:9–13. The Song of Songs is also known as the Song of Solomon and Canticles.
3. Song of Songs 2:10–14.
4. Patai (1990 ed., pages 272–3).
5. Quoted in Patai (1990 ed., page 275).
6. Frankl (1984 ed., pages 50–51).

8

HOD - GLORY

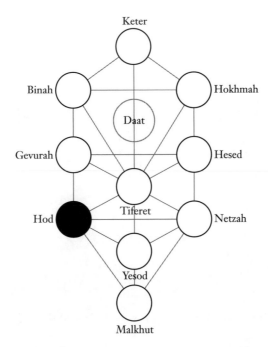

The eighth path is called 'Perfect Consciousness' (Sekhel Shalem).
From it emanate the organizing principles.[1]
Its roots are in the depths of Gedulah (Hesed),
from whose essence it emanates.

SEFER YETZIRAH

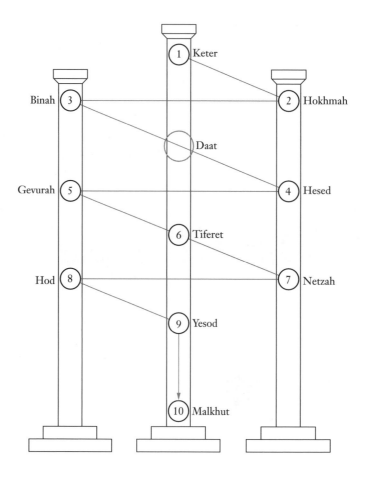

The Three Pillars and the evolution of the sefirot

The sefirah of Hod, Glory or Splendour, is on the left hand side of the Tree of Life, the side known as the 'Pillar of Form'. In Hod, creative ideas become structured plans. The inspirations and intuitions of higher sefirot become manifest as strategies that can be carried out. The *Sefer Yetzirah* text indicates that Hod is closely associated with Hesed. In Hesed we have creative inspiration. In Hod this can be turned into ideas that can in turn be translated into the reality of Malkhut. In Hod, the possibilities conceived in Hesed acquire shape and form. If Hesed is the creative department of the universe, Hod is where those ideas that pass the critical evaluation of Gevurah are thought through. Everything in creation is a thought of the Divine and together these thoughts make up the extraordinary and wondrous thing that is our cosmos and, closer to home, our biosphere the Earth.

In science our understanding of the world of form has deepened greatly over the centuries. Until the invention of the microscope, we could only classify the world around us according to the outer appearance of things. This can be deceptive. We can now analyze the structure of DNA and this has shown us that our biological world is different from what we supposed. For most of the history of science, experts have drawn the tree of life, which maps the path of evolution, by comparing the gross surface features of our planet's life forms. Fungi, for instance, were grouped with plants because they look much like them and grow in one spot, but we now know that fungi have more in common with humans than with plants. We can also trace the origin of the different species that inhabit our world today. We now know, for instance, that all plant life on our planet derived from one particular plant species, which lived originally in salt water, then migrated to freshwater and then to land. Many plants attempted to make the transition to land, but all but one failed. They did not pass the Netzah endurance test. One particular plant did survive and became the mother of all plant species.

The links between Hesed and Hod manifest in many ways. Hesed is associated in Kabbalah with the first day of the seven symbolic days of creation and Hod with the fifth day. On the first day, the waters were made and on the fifth the creatures of the sea. In the Western Mystery Tradition, Hod is associated with the element of water. This may come as a surprise to people versed in astrology, for whom such a thinking state of consciousness must surely be associated with air. Visualize, though, a well in the desert. The air is clean and pure, but hot and dry. There is no pollution because nothing can endure here under the burning sun. Then think of a temple with a pure clear well from which water can be drawn. Think of how refreshing that water would taste after a long trek through the desert and of how it would clear the brain. This is the power of Hod. It gives us clarity and purity of thought. It rids us of woolliness and muddle. It washes away difficulties by showing us a clear and straight way to follow. It brings us to our senses and sobers us up.

In Biblical text, Rachel meets Jacob at *Be'er lakhai ro'i*, 'The Well of Living Visions'.[2] This was the well that revealed to Hagar the future of her son Ishmael and to Rebekah that she would marry Isaac. The waters of the well help us to see clearly and truly. The liquid of Netzah could be said to be wine ruled by the Greek God Dionysus, God of the vine, God of intoxication and wildness. Hod is the sefirah of clear and cold common sense, purity of purpose, and clear vision. This is the sefirah of clear, crystal water and the rationality of the Greek God Apollo. In Hod, we enter the philosophical realm of the lovers of intellectual thought.

Biological life is based on mathematical codes. The coding of DNA differentiates multicellular organisms into different types. The structures and form of matter can be expressed mathematically through numbers. Mathematics and physics are the ultimate Hodic sciences. Hod is the sefirah of scientific determinism. One thing follows another in the universe in orderly and predictable sequence. This rationale was the basis of the development modern science. Nineteenth- and early-20th-century scientists assumed that the universe was a lawful universe with orderly sequences that could be predicted, if only we had sufficient knowledge. Cause and effect was seen as an unbroken and inevitable chain. Laws in all senses – the law of the land, mathematical laws – are Hodic creations. Laws function very well as long as we accept certain assumptions. However, these assumptions are just that: 'assumptions'. They will work well, but only up to a point. We can operate with Newtonian physics when we deal with mechanical machines. Beyond that we need quantum physics, which works with indeterminism not determinism. Hod, like rationality, is limited in its scope. When we get to Chaos Theory we are moving out of Hod's orbit to Yesod.

THE DIVINE IN HOD

The Hebrew Divine name in Hod is *Elohim Tzevaot*, which can be translated as 'Goddess of Hosts', the feminine counterpart of the God of Hosts of Netzah. In the Western Mystery Tradition, deities associated with Hod are those of the mind, such as the Roman Mercury and his Greek equivalent Hermes, both of whom were messengers of the Gods. We also have

Minerva, Goddess of learning and the Nine Graces, the muses who inspired different forms of learning and art. In the Norse pantheon we have Odin in his form as the seeker of knowledge and knower of words of magical power. Ancient Egypt had Thoth, patron of the sacred art of hieroglyphic writing and a patron of magic.

TITLES AND IMAGES

Hod can be translated as 'Splendour' or 'Glory'. What is this glory? In Netzah, we understand the beauty of the created world and the victory of the triumph of the possible. In Hod, we begin to understand the workings of the universe, this complex system that keeps the stars in their places and the planets in their orbits. We understand that it is a truly glorious universe that we are privileged to inhabit. In the Western Mystery Tradition, the image of Hod is that of the Hermaphrodite – a mixture of male and female. Here we realize the potential of the female in the male and the male in the female. We must balance Netzah and Hod.

HOD AND INDIVIDUAL DEVELOPMENT

Netzah is the sefirah of emotional education. Hod is the realm of thinking and we must exercise our Hodic functions when it comes to higher study and work. In Hod, we learn to exercise our rational faculties in order to support ourselves in the world. Hod is necessary for us to enter the adult world. Hod and Netzah, thinking and feeling, in Western society are often thought of respectively as male and female. Similarly, Hodic activity is often associated more with men than with women. Interestingly, Kabbalah has the opposite association, Hod is on the feminine pillar of form and Netzah is on the masculine pillar of force. In any event, in the new millennium, these distinctions may become unimportant. Male and female roles will no longer be so distinct. Birth control and greater awareness of human individuality have allowed women and men to become more themselves. Women are active in what were purely male professions such as academia, medicine, politics and business, and men take a more active role in relationships and parenting. We are less likely to be pushed into a particular occupation or social role purely because of our gender; though there are still social pressures.

RATIONALITY

Hod is the sefirah of the intellect and reason. In Hesed, we have the guru or spiritual teacher. In Hod we have teaching and teachers of another sort. These are the professors and teachers of intellectual knowledge. Hod in the human mind is the power that helps us analyze and categorize. All systems, whether library systems, computer systems or logical categories are associated with Hod. Hod allows us to perceive something, name it, and file it away under the appropriate heading.

In the late 18th century and the 19th century, great store was placed on rationality. Reason was to be our new God. Freudian psychoanalysis, although a treatment for the emotions and a technique for 'clearing out' the unconscious, was for Freud a movement to espouse the rational conscious mind and to rid ourselves of domination by the unconscious. We would learn to control our irrational impulses and childish fantasies. We would 'grow up' to act as logical human beings. Freud hoped that our intellects, the scientific spirit of reason, would come to dominate us, but would allow a due place for expression of our emotions. This seems naively optimistic given that for many people it is not intellectual expression that is problematic – they can express intellectual ideas readily enough. It is emotional expression that many people find difficult. Today, we are in any event much less naïve about the competence of reason and its grip on the human psyche. In search of rationality, Freud himself was very superstitious. He was a practitioner of the complex Kabbalistic art of *Gematria*, which will be familiar to anyone who has seen Darren Aronofsky's 1998 film Π (*Pi*). Gematria analyzes Hebrew words according to their numerology. In Hebrew, each letter is also a number. A word can be given a number based on the sum of its individual letters. Words that have the same sum total are believed to relate to one another and the number of a word will give clues as to its true meaning. For instance, the word *Ahad*, which means Unity, is spelled in Hebrew – Alef (1), Het (8), Dalet (4) = 13. This is also the number of the word Ahebah – Alef (1), He (5), Bet (2), He (5) – which means Love. We can therefore make the interpretation that Love is Unity and Unity is Love. Through *Gematria*, the Torah, the Law, which comprises the first five books of the Bible, and other sacred Hebrew texts, can be read as secret codes. For some Kabbalists, the Torah consists entirely of names of God or, more radically, one name of God. Jewish legend speaks of another woman, who preceded Eve. This was Adam's mysterious first wife, Lilith, a witch–Goddess figure, whose power derived from her knowing the ineffable name of God. The search for the secret name of God is at the heart of Aronofsky's film. The film has some wonderful quotes that illustrate the nature of Hod. At one point, the hero Maximilian Cohen says:

> *11:15 pm, restate my assumptions:*
> 1. *Mathematics is the language of nature.*
> 2. *Everything around us can be represented and understood through numbers.*
> 3. *If you grasp these numbers, patterns emerge.*
> *Therefore: There are patterns everywhere in nature.*

It is in Hod that the patterns of Nature are laid down. Music is also associated with Hod and, in the Western Mystery Tradition, Hod is also associated with the Greek God Apollo, patron of music. Musical and mathematical ability are strongly correlated in the human psyche because music depends on patterns of sound. The ability to listen to music is associated with Hod, as is the ability to write it. To perform requires sensitivity in the feeling realm and here we must return to Netzah to help us. To perform requires passion as well as Hod's technical precision.

THE WORK OF HOD

People whose work is Hodic want to find the truth. Archetypal seekers after scientific truth include the quantum physicist Albert Einstein and Marie Curie, discoverer of radiation treatment who herself succumbed to cancer from exposure to her own nuclear substances, such being the primitive understanding of the dangers of radiation of the period. Hod can also help create the dedicated civil rights lawyer (when infused with the humanitarianism of Hesed), or the tireless scientific worker who spends long hours in her or his laboratory to make a medical break through. When Gevurah infects Hod, however, it might be the latest weapon that the scientist works on rather than medical advances. Hod is morally neutral. A danger is that of rationality untainted by other considerations. Here we descend into the nightmare world of the concentration camp doctors and their 'scientific' experiments. Hod alone can be reason without values. It is Netzah and other sefirotic energies that take us into the realm of balanced decision-making and living. True scientific advance is not the work of Hod alone. Rationality does not help us make the imaginative leap that results in new theory. We need inspiration from elsewhere.

WORD

Hod is not only a sefirah of science. It also relates to communication by the power of the word, both oral and written. Writing has had an enormous influence on human development. We are no longer dependent on our individual memories, as we were for most of *Homo Sapiens'* 500,000-year existence. Instead we can inscribe signs on durable materials and create knowledge that can be transmitted across vast distances or between generations. In our own era, we have evolved electronic data processing. Through computers, modems and Internet networks, we can access and communicate more knowledge than ever before. In Kabbalah, prophecy is said to relate to Hod and Netzah. Prophecy in the sense of original vision is inspired by Hesed but must be made manifest though Hod, the power of the spoken word, enlivened with the passion of Netzah. Hod alone can communicate teachings, but it does not give us original thought. Hod thinks 'within the box'.

The power of the word is conspicuous today in the media. Advertising, film, newspapers and politics rely on manipulating words in order to persuade us to certain ideas, thoughts and ideologies. This power is frequently abused. The Shadow side of Hod is thievery and trickery. The deities associated in the Western Mystery Tradition with Hod include Mercury who is God of thieves and merchants, as well as messenger of the Gods. In politics there are three great powers. One is Hodic, the power of the word. Another is Yesodic, the power of the image. The third is Netzahian, the power of emotional conviction. Politicians and their spin doctors manipulate words, images and emotions to create a product that can be sold to the public. 'Selling' is another keynote of Hod. Mercury is also the patron of transactions and business. Stock markets are Hodic institutions where financial resources can be rationally manipulated. However, irrational forces such as consumer confidence, which may value something way beyond its rational worth, power the markets themselves.

Many women have made their mark in Hodic occupations, such as writing and teaching. On average, women are biologically better with words and language than men. Girls learn to speak, read and write at an earlier age than boys. This gives them the power to communicate at an earlier age and, in an era where jobs are increasingly dependent on communication skills, women are beginning to achieve greater equality in the workplace – which does not mean, of course, that there is not still a long way to go.

EGO AND PERSONALITY

The energies of the lower part of Tiferet, together with Netzah, Hod, and Malkhut, create a centre that represents our Ego. This is the 'I' that we are conscious of on a day-to-day basis. We believe that we are the thoughts, feelings, instincts, sensations and intuitions that we are consciously aware of, but in reality there is much more going on behind this. The Ego is strongly influenced by the True Self in Tiferet, which has purposes that are more long-ranging and can be at variance with those of the Ego. We are also influenced by archetypal energies mediated by Hokhmah, Binah, Hesed and Gevurah.

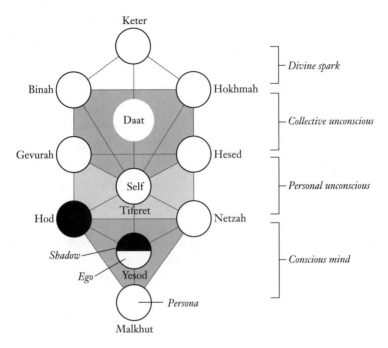

Jungian Tree of Life

Netzah, Hod, Tiferet and Malkhut are the dimensions that influence our everyday personality and the way we present ourselves to the world. Our personalities are unlikely to be influenced equally by all four of these sefirot. Most people are lop-sided in their development and will show characteristics of one or two of the sefirot more than others. In fiction, characters are often stereotypes of particular sefirot. Hod is the sefirah of thinking and, more specifically, of rational, logical, scientific and mathematical thought. The epitome of the Hodic personality was the Vulcan, Mr. Spock in the first *Star Trek* series. His whole life was dictated by logic. Feelings played no part in his world. His mirror image was Dr. McCoy, 'Bones', with whom he was frequently in conflict. Bones was the epitome of the Netzahian feeling function. His primary concern was people. Scotty was the engineer who kept the star ship functioning. His was the Malkhutian world 'down below' in the engine room. Without his intervention, the USS *Enterprise* would have got nowhere. The skills of the three men would not have operated well without the leadership and vision of someone who could co-ordinate them. This was the role of the intuitive Captain Kirk. His leaps of logic helped them solve problems that baffled the rationality of Mr. Spock. Here Captain Kirk was acting as the Tiferetic 'king'. The starship itself was the Yesodic world in which the four men operated.

GUILT AND ANXIETY

Negative thinking can be part of the Shadow side of Hod. We worry and think negative thoughts about ourselves and those around us. Worry and regret damage health. We become and trapped in the past instead of allowing ourselves to use our energy to build the future. Rabbi Shimon of Yaroslav lived to a very old age. When he was asked the secret for achieving the blessing of a long life, he replied:

> *When a person constantly complains about the injustices in the world, and that G-d's management of the world is unfair, he is taken up to the heavens, where he can be shown how and why things happened, and that in the overall scheme of the universe, G-d is indeed just and fair. Since I always accepted the Divine judgment and never complained that G-d was unfair, there was no need to call me up there, and so I was permitted to remain in this world.*[3]

To live long and healthily, we need to be able to let go of negative thoughts. This is not easy. People who are dominated by Hod want to be in control of their environment. Their desks will be orderly; their class notes neat. Their clothes will be practical and functional. Hod eschews the ornamentation beloved of Netzah. The white laboratory coat is a Hodic garment. When we become obsessed with Hod, we get obsessive–compulsive disorder. Hod loves ritual and ceremony and, in the psychiatrically ill, ritual can become a means for controlling the environment. Obsessive–compulsive people are obsessed with cleanliness. They may wash their hands constantly so as not to become contaminated. They may suffer a severe anxiety attack if a book is not placed in exactly the right spot on the bookshelf. Freud made a detailed study of obsessional patients. He believed the obsessions were the result of unresolved problems in childhood development – particularly in what Freud called the 'anal stage' where we learn potty training and how to control our bowel movements. Children at this stage learn to associate being unclean with guilt. Freud believed that many religious purification rituals resembled obsessional attempts to rid ourselves of contamination and guilt.

In Hod, we find religions based on the 'Word' and codified in holy books. Where religions are book-dominated, there will be traditionalists for whom the written word, as mediated by human beings, and the thoughts of God are identical. The human mind under Divine inspiration is believed to be capable of transmitting the thoughts of a transcendent deity. Given the flaws in human make-up, this is an optimistic conclusion.

HODIC QUALITIES

The virtue or positive quality of Hod is truthfulness. Hod and Netzah represent two different types of truth – literal rational truth and poetic or mythic truth. Netzah's truth is the truth of art, which is not to convey the concrete representation of something, but to convey its essence and what a human being might feel about it. Hod's truth is the truth of photography, which is to capture things exactly as they are. Of course, these truths overlap. Art used to be representational but with the scientific advance of photography, it has become more abstract and symbolic. The camera can lie and the skill of photojournalists is to make us see images in the way they choose. Similarly, science often presents a particular value-laden worldview, even when it is masquerading as objective. Netzah is unashamedly subjective and may in its subjectivity show us universal human truths, experiences and values. Hod is rational and strives to be objective, but it may delude itself as to the extent of its objectivity. Hod's negative quality or vice is dishonesty.

SPIRITUAL EXPERIENCE OF HOD

The spiritual experience of Hod is the Vision of Splendour. What is this splendour? The *Sefer Yetzirah* speaks of Hod as 'the Perfect and Absolute Intelligence'. In Hod we realize the ultimate splendour of the perfected mind. The Divine mind has created the laws of the physical universe by which our cosmos, this extraordinary creation that is the Divine's expression of Itself in matter, can operate. Imagine a cosmic vision in which you see the scientific laws of our universe revealed to you. This is the splendour and wonder of the universe. The physical universe is a mechanism of extraordinary ingenuity and balance. Scientists now know that if the law of gravity was even slightly stronger or weaker, planets could not form in stable orbits around stars. Biological life as we know it could not exist. When we grasp the mathematical and scientific improbability of a system such as our cosmos existing at all, then we experience the awe that comes from realizing that we, you and I and all the other human beings who share our world, have roles to play in this wondrous creation.

Prince Louis de Broglie, a French nobleman, received the Nobel Prize for Physics for demonstrating that matter, like light, has wave properties – a discovery that was the foundation for quantum mechanics. He was originally a medieval historian, but turned his considerable intellectual powers to a completely different field because he became excited by the idea of discovering 'the last hiding places of reality'. He began working on his theory because he was attracted to its intellectual beauty. For scientists involved in the Deep Green project, financed by the United States federal government and others to map the 'Tree of Life' of biological life on our planet, it is primarily the sheer intellectual excitement of working out one of Nature's grand designs that is the scientists' driving force. For the dedicated biologist, exploring the inner world of cellular structures is as exciting as painting a new picture is to an artist, or discovering a new planet is to an astro-physicist. The elegance of a refined intellectual idea is part of the Vision of Hod, the Vision of Splendour, that is the driving force of science.

EXPLORING HOD

EXERCISE 1: BRINGING HOD INTO YOUR LIFE

We need Hod energy whenever we have to think clearly and logically, be it sitting an examination, setting up a new computer system, or driving a car.

If we know that we need to engage in a Hodic activity, we can draw on the energy of Hod to help us.

To bring Hod into your life, you need to bring yourself into contact with things associated with Hod. In your home, make an altar to Hod. Cover it with a white cloth and place candlesticks with orange candles on your altar. Orange is the colour associated with Hod in the Western Mystery Tradition and brass is the metal of Hod. Clean brass candlesticks would be perfect. Buy or pick orange flowers to decorate the altar. Just eight will do – the number of Hod. Now add a bowl of pure clear spring water. You might like to find a floating candle of orange for this. You now have a suitable altar for Hod.

Now you must make your home a suitable place for Hodic energy. Hod is a sefirah of organization and form, so tidy up and put away neatly and in categories any papers or business documents that you have. This is a good time to complete financial records or your tax returns. Revenue collection and banking are very Hodic activities. Hod requires filing systems. Hod also requires cleanliness. Clean your home, perhaps using an organic polish such as beeswax rather than a chemical one. Once you have ordered your home, order other aspects of your life. Organize your cupboards. Throw away or give away any items you no longer need. Go through your purse and throw away old supermarket receipts. Organize your books, videos, computer discs and CDs. What about your kitchen? Are its cupboard full of old packages of food that you never quite got around to finishing? If so, get rid of them. Remember Hod requires cleanliness and order to do its work.

Find an oil burner for your altar and burn an aromatherapy oil to cleanse your home and clear your thinking. Lavender is good for this. Now say an invocation to a Hodic aspect of deity. Here, for instance, is an invocation to Hermes.

You are as old as time –
you sprang forth from the first breath taken;
yet you have aged not,
for you are born anew with each gust of wind
and every gentle breeze.

The leaves dancing on the trees
and still water silently mirthful with sudden ripples
show that you pass by.
Fleet of foot with winged heels,
the messenger of the Gods,
with words that all must hear
cascading from your silver tongue;
from the Gods you bring healing,
healing from your magic touch.

You are quicksilver,
you are the wind,
you are Hermes,
the very breath of life.[4]

Before tackling an important Hodic task, prepare your altar, light your altar candles and burn your oil. Meditate in silence for a while and then say the invocation. Now think about what you need to achieve and visualize it. Imagine it happening and coming about. Imagine a clean wind blowing through you and blowing away all your own internal opposition to what you are trying to do. Remember that the mind creates all sorts of barriers and traps for us. Remember that Hod is about boundaries and systems, but that we control the systems and not they us.

EXERCISE 2: RECONCILING THINKING AND FEELING

Hod is prone to anxiety. Hod likes everything to be logical, but unfortunately the world is not like this. Hod is also subject to negative thinking and ideas. Negative thinking becomes a pattern that we find difficult to eliminate. The mind becomes used to running in a particular groove and it takes mental effort to break the boundaries to create new and more positive patterns. See if you can recognize some of these negative thought patterns in yourself.

Anything nice I have will be taken away.
Everyone is against me.
Everything is difficult.
Everything is my fault.
I can never get close to people.
I can never succeed; I'm a failure.
I'm inferior to others; I count for nothing.
I have to do everything myself.
I must never be angry.
I'm not allowed to enjoy myself.
I'm not allowed to have what I want.

Hod is a judgemental sefirah. We can find ourselves in the position of not only constantly judging everything but, what is even worse, constantly judging everything negatively. Negative beliefs are hard to dislodge because they are survival strategies designed to help us get through life. At some point in our childhood or early adulthood we will have found them temporarily useful and they will have stuck. These types of mistaken beliefs distort the way we live and interact with others. This does not mean we have to stick with them. We can change. To change Hod we need the opposite energy, Netzah. Similarly, to change Netzah, we need the opposite energy, Hod.

One of the difficult arts for human beings is balance. Most of us are lopsided in our development and lean towards thinking or feeling, Hod or Netzah, as our main way of judging what goes on in the world. This is an exercise to help us find a point of balance. The exercise is an inner journey. It will take about an hour. You will need to be alone in a quiet dimly-lit room where you can relax. You could type or write the instructions so that you can refer to them one by one. Alternatively you could record them onto a cassette with pauses in between to perform the visualization. Have some paper and coloured pens to record your experiences and help you remember them.

1. Relax and settle into a regular pattern of breathing. With each out breath, breathe out tension. Relax the muscles that hold tension. When you breathe in, breathe in the energy of life.

2. Imagine you are walking along a road. The sun is overhead and there is water nearby. Become aware of the road – what is its scenery, its atmosphere, the time of day, the feel and smell of the place?

3. You sense that you are about to meet someone who represents your analytical mind, the thinking part of your psyche. Your thinking self begins to come into view. You approach one another and stop to greet one another. You begin to talk. Listen to what your thinking self has to say. Note the appearance of your thinking self. Is he or she old or young, female or male, strong or weak, well nourished or under nourished? Now see if you can tell why your thinking self should come to you in this form. Why should it appear to you in this way at this time?

4. When you are ready, prepare to move on, but before moving on ask your thinking self to accompany you on the next stage of your journey.

5. As you continue your journey along the road, you sense you are about to meet someone or something that represents your feeling self. The feeling self begins to come into view. You stop and greet one another. You begin to talk. Listen to what your feeling self has to say and note the appearance of your feeling self. Is he or she old or young, female or male, strong or weak, well nourished or under nourished? Now see if you can tell why your feeling self should come to you in this form. Why should it appear to you in this way at this time?

6. When you are ready, end this discussion. Before moving on, invite both your thinking and feeling selves to accompany you on the next stage of your journey.

7. You continue along your way and find yourself approaching a sacred place where you can commune with your True Self. Allow an image of your True Self to come into your mind. Settle yourself comfortably with your True Self and together explore the relationship between your thinking and feeling selves and the parts they play in your life. Explore any difficulties there are and any changes needed to produce a creative and positive balance between them that will allow for further development of each.

8. In this sacred place, Hod, your thinking self, and Netzah, your feeling self, can come together creatively in the presence of your wiser True Self in Tiferet. A new potential of wholeness or synthesis may be

born. Allow your imagination to offer you a symbol for this wholeness or synthesis.

9. When you are ready, return slowly into consciousness and into your room, bringing with you the symbol, or sense of energy of this synthesis and potential.

10. Relax and then, when you are ready, anchor the experience by drawing your thinking self, your feeling self and your True Self. Draw also the road along which you travelled, the sacred place where you communed with your different selves, and the symbol of synthesis that came to you at the end. Anchoring your experience in drawing will help you find that synthesis in your outer life.

TO YESOD

We are nearing the end of our journey. We have seen the power of mind. Let us now turn to Yesod, Foundation, the animal world.

Hod – Splendour

Title: Glory, Splendour
Image: Hermaphrodite

Divine Aspect

Hebrew Divine Name: *Elohim Tzevaot* – Goddess of Hosts
Deities in other traditions: Nine Muses (Greek Goddesses of arts and sciences), Mercury (Roman God of learning), Hermes (Greek God of learning and magic), Thoth (Egyptian God of learning, writing and magic), Odin (Norse God – as discoverer of the runes), Apollo (Greek God of music).
Spiritual Paths: Greek philosophy, 'Religions of the Book'

Correspondences in the Physical Universe

In the Cosmos: Kokab (Mercury)
Number: 8
Colour: Orange

Correspondences in Humankind

Spiritual experience: Vision of Splendour
Positive quality: Honesty, truthfulness
Negative quality: Dishonesty
In the human body: Right hip and leg

Notes

1. Also translated as 'preparation of principles', 'original arrangement'.

2. Genesis 16:7–15.

3. Twerski, Abraham J. (1992) *Living Each Week*, Mesorah Publications (page 454). Orthodox
   Jews prefer not to write down the full name of God and, in English, write G-d.

4. *Hermes*, Chris Crowley, (1985).

9

YESOD –
FOUNDATION

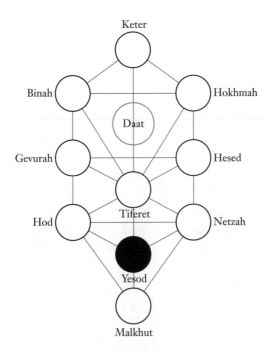

Keter

Binah

Hokhmah

Daat

Gevurah

Hesed

Hod

Tiferet

Netzah

Yesod

Malkhut

The Ninth Path is called 'Pure Consciousness' (Sekhel Tahor)
because it purifies the sefirot.
It tests and corrects their design,
and unifies them with its essence,
so that they may not be destroyed or divided.
SEFER YETZIRAH

Yesod's realm is that of animal consciousness. We know that animals are largely controlled by their instinctual lives – sex, territorial protection, guarding and rearing of young, the need for food, drink and shelter. We too share these drives. Higher mammals also engage in more sophisticated activities. They play and they experience pleasure and pain. A cat will calculate which humans are friendly to it and which are not, which will provide food and sensory pleasure from stroking and which humans will drive it away. Higher animals have memories and can learn from experience. Our ape cousins even use simple tools. They are aware of their surroundings. At dawn, baboons sit together in silent watchfulness, their paws raised to the rising sun. The transition that the human animal made was to reach up from our Yesod state to pluck the fruit of the Tree of Knowledge. A new cycle of evolution began, almost as important as that made with the creation of the cosmos from Keter and of biological life from Tiferet.

THE DIVINE IN YESOD

The Hebrew Divine name in Yesod is *Shaddai El Hai*, the Mighty Living One, or the Divine Life Force. The name *El Shaddai*, which can be translated as the All Sufficient God, also appears in Genesis 17:1. 'Shad' means 'breast' in Hebrew. Like a nursing mother, the Divine, the source of our being, succours humankind and takes care of our needs. Here we are close to physical manifestation and the Divine is at its most powerful.

In terms of correspondences to the human body, Yesod corresponds to the penis. Semen and menstrual blood are other important symbols. The archetypal image of Yesod is that of a beautiful and strong young man. Yesod represents the animal side of ourselves. Early religions often worshipped the Divine in animal form. For our early ancestors, everything in Nature was a reflection of the Divine. To them animals such as the otter, bear, stag, elk, lion or eagle seemed closer to the strength and beauty that they imagined belonged to the Divine than did the human form. Some traces of the veneration of Gods in animal form are found in the Israelites' occasional lapses into worshipping the Golden Calf and in Christianity in the worship of Christ as the lamb. The Divine of course is beyond images, but Yesodic images are symbols that can help us realize deeper truths. This

aspect of the Divine is Lord or Lady of the Beasts who cares for the animal kingdom.

Deities that relate to Yesod are those of the Moon, the planet associated with Yesod, and those associated with the power to change the shape of matter. It is important to understand that the Israelites did not become monotheistic Yahweh worshippers overnight. Many other deities from other inhabitants of Palestine, such as the Canaanites, struggled with Yahweh for the hearts and minds of the people. In particular, Goddess worship won hearts and minds in Judaism, even as it did in Catholicism through the Virgin Mary. Asherah was a Mesopotamian Moon Goddess worshipped by Israelite women in particular, who offered her cakes at full Moon. Figurines of Asherah are found through the Biblical period, at all levels of society. One inscription on Mount Sinai indicates that both Asherah and Yahweh were worshipped together. The family of Leah and Rachel, the wives of Jacob, lived in Haran, a city that remained Pagan until the 11th century. Haran was the birthplace of Asherah who was also worshipped as Ishtar of the Babylonians and Inanna of the Sumerians. Other famous Biblical women such as Rebekah and Sarah were from families of priestesses who served the Moon Goddess.[1] In the Roman pantheon, the moon deity was the Goddess Diana, who was also Mistress of the Animals and a Hunter Goddess. Greece had Selene and also Hecate, a Goddess of witchery and storms.

There were also lunar Gods, such as Ishtar's son Tammuz. Thoth was an Egyptian God who was associated with the Moon in his capacity as a recorder of time. Yesod is the sefirah that is associated with calendars. The earliest calendars were lunar, measuring time by lunar nights rather than solar days – as the Jewish calendar still does today. In the Norse pantheon we have Odin in his guise as Shaman and Shape-shifter. We also have Greek Adonis who was renowned for his physical beauty and takes us back to the image of a beautiful naked man.

The Moon gives us some clues about Yesod's relationship to Malkhut. The Moon has an invisible gravitational pull on our Earth and affects all water on our planet. This includes the tides and liquids within the human body. The Moon affects menstruation in women who do not live with modern electric light that interferes with the Moon's regulation of the cycle. It marks the times and tides of reproduction. The Moon also affects other bleeding and the speed with which blood clots. In a similar way, Yesod acts as an invisible influence on Malkhut. Yesod is associated with the element of ether, which in the Western Mystery Tradition is a force that binds matter together. We could understand it better in modern terms as a non-visible physical property of matter. Gravitational pull that holds the universe together is another image.

TITLES AND IMAGES

In some early Kabbalistic texts, the ninth sefirah is called 'All' rather than Yesod, Foundation. If you look at Yesod's position on the Tree of Life, you will see that it precedes Malkhut, the material world. Everything, all that is to manifest in Malkhut, pre-exists in Yesod. In the Western Mystery Tradition, Yesod is also called 'The Treasure House of Images'. Before we create anything we have an image of it, whether visual, olfactory, verbal, or other sound. It exists within us before it exists outwardly. Often new ideas in both art and science come to us in the form of images. They arrive into our consciousness via the unconscious and it is then the work of the conscious rational mind in Hod to analyze them; to test them out and find their flaws. Great scientists have frequently dreamed their important discoveries. Breakthroughs have come in the form of dream imagery in the world of the night. It has then been the task of the scientist to use his or her scientific training and theoretical knowledge to see if the intuitive knowledge that has arrived, as it were, down the Middle Pillar of Consciousness on the Tree of Life, is correct and factual. Quite often such knowledge is shown to be right – it holds up to the tests of Malkhut – but it does not fit the theory of the day. Galileo knew that the world was round, even if the scientific theories of his time told him this was nonsense.

Yesod is strongly related to the dream world. The *Sefer Yetzirah* text tells us that a purification process goes on in Yesod. Some forms are brought into manifestation at Malkhut. Others never get beyond the prototype stage. It is as though the Divine mind dreams us all into existence. Some of those dreams become reality and some do not because they cannot pass the test of reality. When we pass out of the body again in death, our image form in this incarnation still exists in Yesod. It is this that becomes a ghost if we have suffered trauma and cannot let go of the past to move forward into new incarnation.

Hindu mythology tells us that our material world is all Maya, illusion, a kind of dream from which we will eventually awaken to see true reality. Yesod is like the dream of the Divine that contains images of all that is to be created. The different images come into being for a time and then fade away. A more modern image would be that of a long movie. Our universe is like a full-length feature production dreamt up by the creative mind of the Divine. Eventually the story will end and another will begin. A difference between the story of our universe and other stories is that the plot is not fully written. The Divine has created the scenario and characters and allowed them to create the story as they go along. This is called free will. The Divine Itself can see the end, because the Divine exists outside of time and all things are simultaneously present; but by breaking off different bits of Its consciousness and isolating them, they can interact together independently of one another. Thus in our own lives we can act independently and interact with others acting independently. This creates infinite permutations of possibilities and events and thus there is randomness and a freedom in what is created.

YESOD AND THE BODY

The magical image of Yesod is of a strong and beautiful naked man. A modern example might be an athlete or body builder. Gay culture has always revered the male form but, in the 19th and much of the 20th centuries, for heterosexual men to focus on adornment or on making their bodies beautiful objects was seen as suspect. Fortunately, this is changing. Men are now much more aware of their health and appearance. We can thus experience once more the sensual joy of the male body as did the Lady of the *Song of Songs*.

> *Listen! My lover! Look!*
> *Here he comes,*
> *leaping across the mountains, bounding over the hills;*
> *my lover is like a gazelle or a young stag. ...*

My lover is radiant and ruddy, outstanding among ten thousand.
His head is purest gold; his hair is wavy and black as a raven.
His eyes are like doves by the water streams,
washed in milk, mounted like jewels.
His cheeks are like beds of spice yielding perfume.
His lips are like lilies dripping with myrrh.
His arms are rods of gold set with chrysolite.
His body is like polished ivory decorated with sapphires.
His legs are pillars of marble set on bases of pure gold.
His appearance is like Lebanon, choice as its cedars.
His mouth is sweetness itself; he is altogether lovely.
This is my lover, this my friend, O daughters of Jerusalem.[2]

In our health-conscious age, having a body that is strong as well as beautiful is also a concern for women. Many of us suffer now not from the diseases of poverty, but from those of Western civilization – too much food of the wrong sort and lack of exercise. Health is not just about the physical body. Associated with Yesod is the etheric body. This contains the energy centres of the body, often known as the chakras. These are important for bodily health, but more is known about them in the East than the West. Eastern martial arts depend on the right flow of Qi energy in the body. When a kung fu master directs Qi into a particular body part, it can become impervious to pain and can have an extraordinary resistance to physical force. We can see this in martial arts demonstrations. Understanding etheric energy can enhance physical strength.

SHAMANISM

Yesod as the realm of images is the realm of the shaman who journeys into other 'worlds' or states of consciousness. Shamans are in touch with the animal kingdom and understand the ways of species other than their own. In older societies, shamans guided hunters to their prey. We tend to think of shamanism as the province of the Earth-based and indigenous traditions, but shamanic elements are found in many different religious traditions, including Kabbalah. Shamanism is remarkably widespread. It seems that peoples in many different cultures discovered techniques for voyaging in the country of the mind. In Kabbalistic terms, Shamanism operates in the realm between Malkhut and the higher sefirot, drawing on images from Yesod. There are a number of ways of achieving a Yesodic state of consciousness. In some cultures, hallucinogenic drugs are used. Another method is rhythmic drumming. The shaking of grain in a sieve has been used. Amongst Hasidim, it is common to rock one's body backwards and forwards during prayer to induce ecstasis. The movements to some extent simulate physical movements involved in sexual orgasm. The 18th-century founder of the Hasidic movement, Polish folk healer Israel son of Eliezer (1700–1760), who was known as the Baal Shem Tov, Master of the Divine Name, or Besht for short, taught that for the male devotee:

A prayer constitutes copulation with the Divine (as the Divine Feminine, the Shekhinah) and is similar to the rocking (back and forth) which occurs during the beginning of copulation. So one must rock oneself during the beginning of prayer and then one may stand still and one shall be attached to the Divine in great ecstasy (devkhut). And from the power of rocking oneself, one will reach great awakening.[3]

In Kabbalah and Jewish mysticism, there are many examples of shamanic figures who travel into different worlds, although the word 'shaman' is not usually applied to them. In Jewish tradition, most reference to journeying between different spiritual worlds can be found in the *Merkavah* mystical writings. These were the early precursors to Kabbalistic literature. The *Merkavah*[4] is the Throne Chariot of God. In the Bible, the prophet Ezekiel describes his vision of the *Merkavah* (Ezekiel:1). If you are familiar with the tarot, the Chariot card is a similar image. In the *Merkavah*, the spiritual seeker undertakes a shamanic journey and ascends into the Upper Worlds riding in the Chariot. During the period of Second Temple (*c.* 538 BCE–70 CE) an esoteric doctrine of Genesis and the first chapters of Ezekiel came into existence. The doctrine is now only in scattered fragments known as the *Hekhalot* books. The *Book of Enoch* is one of the more famous. Enoch was a shoemaker who because of his great piety was taken into heaven by God and became the archangel Metatron, the Prince of the Malkhut. The *Hekhalot* writings passed through Jewish converts to Christianity into the

Gnostic tradition and have strongly influenced Kabbalah. The writings contain descriptions of the heavenly palaces or halls (*Hekhalot*) through which we must pass if we are to make the journey to the Divine. The principal speaker in the *Greater Hekhalot* is Rabbi Ishmael who describes a journey through the seven palaces beyond the seven heavens. There are also descriptions of the secret names and seals the initiate needs to combat the demons that guard each portal. The descriptions are presented as discussions between the traveller and the gatekeepers. The structure is similar to mystical journeys found in shamanic cultures of South America, and in the *Books of the Dead* in ancient Egypt and in Tibetan Buddhism, where Buddhism is grafted on to indigenous Bon shamanism.

YESOD AND THE PARANORMAL

The shamanic world encompasses powers of the psyche that are today little understood and which we think of as paranormal. The concept of Yesod is very similar to that found in other traditions: that there is an interconnecting web of energy linking everything in the universe. The rationale of Shamanism and magic is inter-connectedness, a oneness of being. Moses de Leon wrote in *Sefer ha-rimmon*:

> *Everything is linked with everything else down to the lowest ring on the chain, and the true essence of God is above as well as below, in the Heavens and on Earth, and nothing exists outside Him ... Meditate on these things and you will understand that God's essence is linked and connected with all worlds, and that all forms of existence are linked and connected with each other, but derived from His existence and essence.*[5]

Everything, animate and inanimate, is interconnected. Every apparently separate thing, whether rock or plant, human or animal, activity or event, is linked. All things are part of a greater whole and communicate with one another. The apparent separateness of things – people, objects, and events – is an illusion. This is the world view of our earliest ancestors. Nineteenth-century science dismissed these ideas as primitive superstition, but they have been revived by modern science through Chaos Theory, which would be better called 'Unpredictability Theory'. The classic example is how, by a chain of cause and effect, the flapping of a butterfly's wings on one continent can result in meteorological catastrophe on another continent. This is not true chaos because everything is interconnected. Yesod binds everything with everything else, so that chaos cannot occur. What interconnectedness does mean is that a slight change in one part of our cosmos can result in unforeseen changes in another part. A small action of ours might result in unforeseeable chains of cause and effect. It is rather like fiddling with one's computer. We try a command to see what it does and we cause a chain reaction that we cannot undo.

Interconnectedness allows us to consider the possibility of telepathy and clairvoyance. At deeper levels of consciousness, the human mind operates outside the time/space parameters that hold good for material reality. We enter a world in which 'meaningful coincidence' or *synchronicity* occurs. When we are so deeply connected with the unconscious that we are in touch with the True Self at Tiferet, then our psyches can transcend the usual time/space boundaries. We become open to synchronistic events. Synchronicity and clairvoyant dreaming are spontaneous transmissions from this deeper level of the psyche. Inner journeying is a way of consciously tuning in to seek information.

YESOD AND INDIVIDUAL DEVELOPMENT

In human development, Yesod is related to reproduction. It is the stage when we become parents and pass on our human genes to create another person. In some Kabbalistic schools, it was not permitted to study Kabbalah or to seek a mystical return to the Divine, until we had experienced all the realities of our biological selves, including parenting. Human reproduction replicates the Divine's creation of humankind. At this stage, we grow up a bit more. All being well, we realize our responsibilities and the world becomes a more serious place. Not everyone chooses to reproduce physically. We may choose to reproduce through our creative talents or to contribute to society in other ways.

SEX DRIVES

Returning to the magical image of Yesod – a strong and beautiful naked man – whereas Netzah relates to sexual love, Yesod is concerned with sexuality's animalistic end, reproduction. Sexual reproduction has nothing to do with love. It does have much to do with physical attraction and those mysterious entities pheromones, which are hormones that make us attractive to one another. Sexuality for sex's sake is also a function of Yesod; as is the exploitation of sex. Pornography is about manipulation of images. We are presented with images of women and men with their sexual characteristics – hair, muscles, breasts, genitals – exaggerated to 'turn us on'. No real person can ever live up to these images and one of the dangers of pornography is that we may learn to prefer the fantasy to the real thing. Prostitution is also an aspect of the Yesod image. Physical satisfaction is sold without the emotional involvement of Netzah-type sexual love.

INSTINCTS AND HABITS

Yesod is associated with urges caused by hormonal fluctuations. One such urge is the 'nesting instinct' that, for women, makes us at certain times of our lives more likely to seek a partner and to get pregnant. Many women who are convinced that they do not want children feel strong urges to get pregnant as they enter their thirties, when hormones are signalling 'now is your last chance'. These patterns of animal instinctive behaviour are part of Yesodic consciousness.

At Yesod the physical and emotional interact to produce patterns, templates, habits and instincts. Habits are the most problematic of all. It is as though energy becomes accustomed to running in a certain groove and it is then very difficult to change the pattern. This is the realm of drug addiction whereby our interaction with something outside ourselves – a 'hard' drug for instance, 'rewires' our neural circuits permanently so that our bodies no longer function effectively without the presence of the drug. Yesod is the source of desires and cravings. What starts as Netzahian pleasure seeking can end as Yesodic physiological addiction. The instinctual drives of humankind for food, sleep and sex are part of the Yesodic world.

In a well-developed human being, the spirit in Tiferet, the feelings in Netzah and rational thought in Hod will direct these. Where we do not develop into mature adulthood, then Yesodic instincts will control us.

YESOD AND THE SILVER SCREEN

Yesod is the realm of fantasy. Fantasy can be fun, but it can also be something we turn to when outer life is unsatisfactory. Fantasy reflects unfulfilled needs. What Yesod is reflecting therefore are deficiencies in other areas of our personal 'Tree'. Fantasy can be productive or unproductive depending on how we use it. Yesod, in the form of the visual media and their glittering images, dominates our world. Cinema is about dream, fantasy and image. It presents life to us, but not quite as we know it. This is life neatly packaged and parcelled in glorious Technicolor. Through images we can experience vicariously what we cannot access in physical reality. We travel this world and even beyond into the realms of outer space. We live other lives, not our own. We can indulge our fantasies and our dreams.

In Yesod, time can be compressed. Through the moving image we can experience a whole period of history in two and a half hours, including adverts. We can sink into our seats and eat our popcorn while the world is presented to us on a screen. The world of multi-media computing takes us even further into the realm of Yesod. We move into virtual reality. We do not need to learn how to drive a fast car. We can experience it in front of our screens by computer simulation. Through e-mail and the Internet, we can have simulated relationships. Friendships and love affairs can be conducted without the messy business of physically meeting. Once the idea of living by remote control seemed like a sci-fi fantasy. In the 21st century, it is happening. Through the Yesodic world, we can experience reality, but only up to a point. Another problem with the world of the media is that it is a sanitized version of reality. We see the violence but do not experience the pain. We experience sexuality but do not have the complications of building human relationships. The fantasy can divorce us from the reality.

YESODIC QUALITIES

The virtue of Yesod is independence. Independence implies physical independence – that we can support ourselves and earn our living. It also means psychological independence – that we are not totally dependent on others for our self-esteem and that we can rely on our own evaluation. Independence of mind means clarity of thought. Therapists such as Freud and Jung have demonstrated how much goes on beneath the surface of the conscious mind. We are strongly influenced by instincts – love and hate, affiliation and aggression – and by the personal unconscious, in which lurk repressed thoughts, feelings and images that influence the way we behave. Yesod is the sefirah of these hidden drives and complexes that influence our behaviour without our knowledge. One of the goals of adulthood is to become aware of them and to free ourselves of them.

IDLENESS

Our computer world has increased our independence. With our modems on, we can roam alone in the virtual universe. We can access knowledge without the assistance of others. We can live in the self-contained fortress of our individual homes. The vice of Yesod is obvious when you start to think about the life of the average computer nerd. It is idleness. The temptation of Yesod is to live a vicarious life and to do nothing whatsoever. When fantasy can be so much better than reality, the temptation is to fall into a life where we do nothing at all. Masturbation is easier than sexual relationships and Internet relationships are easier than making conversation. We can forget the importance of Malkhut. We learn to dream rather than to act.

SPIRITUAL EXPERIENCE OF YESOD

The spiritual experience of Yesod is the Vision of the Machinery of the Universe. This is a vision of the processes that underlie the existence of our universe. Much of the way that we normally perceive the universe is illusory. When we have a Vision of the Machinery of the Universe we gain insight into its true nature. When we look at the night sky we see an emptiness filled with planets and stars, but the dark spaces are not empty. They are full of what physicists call 'dark matter'. This is the dark remnant of stars, black holes and particles as yet unknown to physics. This matter has not made it to full manifestation in our version of the reality of Malkhut. Dark matter fills more than ninety per cent of the universe. Dark matter is not only out there in space. It is all around us. Scientists can detect its existence because of the tiny magnetic interactions of its particles and its effect on gravitational fields. Our universe is a mechanism, a machine of extraordinary fine-tuning and balance. The Yesodic Vision of the Machinery of the Universe is an experience and not an intellectual appreciation as in Hod. It is a transformation of consciousness. It is the vision which Jewish theologian Martin Buber talked of as an intense emotional experience whereby, despite our ordinary sensate experience being fragmented, we perceive the fundamental unity of life. Normally our brains are rather like fragmented disk drives. All the relevant file components are there, but laid down in haphazard order. The Vision of the Machinery of the Universe defragments the disk drive and we see whole patterns again. This takes us back to the alternative title for Yesod, All.

EXPLORING YESOD

EXERCISE 1: LEVANAH, THE MOON

In the Western Mystery Tradition, Yesod the sefirah of the Moon has the image of a beautiful naked man. This derives from early Near- and Middle-Eastern tradition which saw the Moon as masculine and the Sun as feminine. In German, where nouns have gender, the Moon is still masculine and the Sun feminine. No sefirah is completely masculine or feminine and this is an exercise to explore the feminine side of Yesod. It is an exercise to meet with the Goddess of the Moon and to discover what role She might play in your life. The exercise takes up to an hour. You will need to be alone in a quiet room. If it is daytime, shut out any bright light. At night have only soft, unobtrusive lighting or candlelight. You will need some plain paper and a pen to write and some coloured pens or pencils to draw. You could write or type the exercise in large script so that you can see it by dim lighting. Alternatively, you could read it onto a cassette so you can play it back to yourself. If you read it onto a cassette leave gaps for visualization between each instruction.

1. Close your eyes and take a few moments to relax. Once you are relaxed, imagine it is a summer evening. You are in a wide green and grassy field. The sun has already set and the sky above you is a dark blue. There is a path across the field that leads to a wood. You cross the field towards the wood.

2. Above you the sky grows darker, and a full moon rises, bathing the field and woodland with silver light. There is a feeling of gentleness and peace.

3. The moonlight illuminates the path through the woodland. You follow the path through the trees. You hear the sound of owls, and rabbits come out to play, running and leaping through the trees, their fur silver in the moonlight.

4. The path begins to broaden out into a clearing bathed in moonlight. You sense that the rabbits are gathering around the edge, waiting for something. And then you realize that there are other people present. They are an ancient people in ancient dress. You realize that they are aware of your presence but that you are welcome here, as are all those who come with an open heart.

5. A figure appears from out of the trees and enters the clearing. She is female. On her head is a silver crown or headband. She wears a cloak, but beneath this she is naked and her body shines in the moonlight. She is glorious in her beauty and majesty and at one with the woodland about her. She is the Lady of Life, Queen of the Moon and Lady of the Woods. You sense a great power emanating from her and a great love.

6. As you look at the Lady of the Moon, you become aware that she has sensed your presence, but you are not afraid. You know that you are welcome in this kingdom.

7. You are separated from her by aeons of time and culture, but although

your languages are different, you find that you can sense her thoughts. It is as though she is whispering in your ear and speaking to you alone. She is calling you to come to her.

8. One by one people are entering the circle and approaching the Lady. They are taking gifts to her. You sense too that she is waiting for you to go to her. You become aware that you too have a gift that you wish to give her.

9. You cross the clearing towards her. You are unafraid. You find yourself standing beside the Lady. She emanates great wisdom. She knows about the rhythms of life, of hunter and hunted, of life and death. She knows of the passionate mating lust and of the love for a newborn. She knows all the joys and sorrows that are the lot of physical incarnation. You offer her your gift and you sense that she acknowledges it. Then she seems to want you to draw closer. You reach out and place your hand in hers.

10. You stand together, and in your mind you ask, 'What do I mean to you? How can you help me? How can you heal me? What role can you play in my life?' Pictures form in your mind of your relationship to this feminine energy and power. You sense that its energy is part of your own nature – though deeply hidden. You sense that it is within all women you meet, even though buried by the conditioning of a different society. You stand for a while and allow her to tell you all that she feels you need to know.

11. You may feel there is a question that you wish to ask the Lady about your relationships or your life's journey. If so, ask. Then it is time to withdraw.

12. The sky is getting light and dawn is approaching. Your time together is ending. The Lady bids you farewell. Then you realize that she has a gift for you. You take it and thank her for it.

13. You leave the woodland clearing and find yourself walking through the trees to the field beyond. The sun is rising. You reach the field as the first rays of morning sun are beginning to warm the grass and dry the dew.

14. In your own time, find yourself back in your room. Take a little time to return to everyday reality if you need it.

15. Make notes on your experiences. Write down any thoughts that come

to you. Perhaps draw or paint what you have seen. Here are some questions to help you:

- What was the pathway like which took you to the Goddess? Was it easy or hard?
- How did the Goddess appear to you: old or young, beauty or crone, or maybe all or none of these?
- What do you seek from the Goddess? How can she heal you? How can she help you? What part can she play in your life?
- What gift did she give you? What gift did you give to her?

EXERCISE 2: NOTICING OUR PATTERNS

Yesod relates to moods. Many of our moods relate to things to do with the body. Our eating and drinking patterns, as well as any prescription or other drugs we take, will all affect our moods. Try keeping a mood diary for a month to get in touch with your bodily moods. Divide the day into four – morning, afternoon, evening and night. Note down everything you eat, drink, and any drugs you take. Note your sleep pattern and how long you sleep and whether you dream. All these physiological patterns are part of your personal Yesod and affect how you interact with Malkhut, as well as how clear your thinking (Hod) is, and your emotional balance (Netzah). Also record in your mood diary, your emotional state during each part of the day and anything that triggers a change.

At the end of the month, look back and see if you can distinguish any patterns. Are there phases in your hormonal cycle when you feel more vulnerable, less robust, more likely to lose your temper, irritable for no reason? Once we have noted these patterns and become aware of when they are likely to occur we cannot cease to experience the hormonal fluctuations, but we can change how we react to them. We can learn to detach ourselves and become independent of them. Remember Exercise 1 in Chapter 1, where we said, 'I am not my body'. Similarly, we can say, 'I am not my moods. I have moods and am aware of them. Sometimes I give in to them; sometimes I do not. I don't always have a choice but often I do.' Thus we return to the gift of free will.

EXERCISE 3: MENSTRUATION – AN EXERCISE FOR WOMEN

Menstruation has for many women been associated with negative images. Orthodox Judaism has laws of menstrual purity, which mean that sex and some social contact is forbidden at this time. The Babylonian *Talmud*,[6] or oral Law, dating from 400–500 CE, teaches that if a menstruating woman walks between two men, one of them will die. These types of taboos and folklore teach women to be ashamed about what should be joyous. This is an exercise to explore your feelings about and attitudes towards menstruation.

1. Sit in a quiet room in a meditative position. You might like to light some candles and burn some aromatherapy oil.
2. Think back to your later childhood and early adolescence:
   - What did your mother teach you about menstruation and sex?
   - Did she give you negative messages about women's periods?
   - Did she describe her labour when you were born?
   - Was this described as something joyful or terrible?
   - What messages were there about sex and childbirth – that it was good and joyful, guilt ridden, painful or unpleasant?
3. What about touching?
   - Was this encouraged?
   - Were there kisses and hugs?
   - Alternatively, were you pushed away and told that such things were childish?
4. Think back to when you had your first period. Was this a shock, or were you expecting it?
   - Who told you about periods – your mother, sister, school friends, teachers?
   - What emotions were associated with the early experiences of periods: were you glad: they signified you were now a woman? Were you unhappy at the loss of freedom and restrictions they imposed? Did they seem dirty, unpleasant or impure in some way?
5. Were there any religious taboos that you had to keep when having your periods? Do you keep them still? If you have stopped following

religious taboos, how do you feel about this – pleased or guilty? Do you have sex when menstruating or do your or your partner feel this is 'unclean'?

6. If you find that you have negative ideas about menstruation, think now about how you could begin to change them. What is the joyous side of menstruation? Think about the rest it can offer women, the confidence that the cycle of fertility is functioning well, and the often welcome news that we are not pregnant.

7. Your early conditioning will have given you all kinds of impressions about your body and its pleasantness/unpleasantness, worthiness/ unworthiness and about the value of women and hence of yourself. Think about the questions above. If you have been given negative messages, think about how you can begin to change them to ensure that your daughter or other women that you love, teach, supervise, or train, are not given the same messages. Negative programming can be a self-perpetuating cycle that is damaging to us all – female and male.

TO MALKHUT

We are now coming to our destination, the kingdom, Malkhut, the culmination of the journey of the evolution of the Divine. All endings are only beginnings on another point. At Malkhut we turn on the spiral, a new beginning from the end.

Yesod – Foundation

Titles: Foundation, All, Treasure House of Images, Tzaddik – Righteous One
Image: A strong and beautiful naked man

Divine Aspect

Hebrew Divine Name: *Shaddai El Hai* – Mighty Living One or Divine Life Force

Deities in other traditions: Diana (Roman Virgin Goddess); Hecate (Greek Goddess of witchery and storms); Adonis (Greek God); Tammuz (Babylonian God associated with the Moon), Thoth (Egyptian God – in his aspect as the recorder of time); Odin (Norse) as Shaman and Shape-shifter

Spiritual Paths: Shamanism, animism

Correspondence in the Physical Universe

In the cosmos: Levanah (the Moon)
Number: 9
Colour: Violet

Correspondence in Humankind

Spiritual Experience: Vision of the Machinery of the Universe
Positive Quality: Independence
Negative Quality: Idleness
In the body: Penis

Notes

1. Savina Teubal (1984).

2. Song of Songs 2:8–9, 5:10–16.

3. Based on the translation of Mordechai Rotenberg (1997 page 82).

4. Sometimes written *Merkabah* or *Makava*.

5. Gershom Scholem (1976 ed.).

6. *Babylonian Tractate* IIIa.

MALKHUT –
SOVEREIGNTY

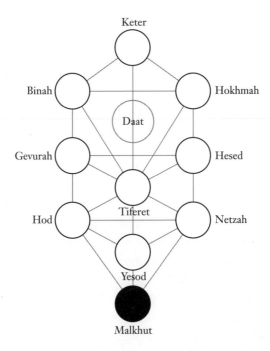

The tenth path is called 'Sparkling Consciousness' (Sekhel MitNotzetz),[1]
because it elevates itself and is enthroned in Understanding (Binah).
It shines with the radiance of all the planets and stars
and emanates the power of the principle of form.

SEFER YETZIRAH

The tenth sefirah is Malkhut, Sovereignty or Kingdom. Malkhut is the Earthly realm. The Hebrew word for earth is *adamah*, which gave its name to the first human, Adam. The creation myth speaks of Adam as being both female and male and fashioned by the Divine from earth or clay. Of course, this may be symbolically true, but we know it cannot be biologically true. However, symbolically the myth emphasizes that we are born of the Earth and our bodies are part of her biosphere. She is part of us and we of her. Often the Earthly realm is looked down upon by spiritual traditions who seek nothing better than to flee the extraordinary gift of life in the human body. This is short-sighted because Malkhut is the final realization of the Divine plan for creation. On our Earthly plane is all that the Divine mind could conceive or create. Humankind is the culmination of that creation: animals with self-awareness. In Malkhut is the final sacred marriage of matter and spirit as incarnate within each one of us is a particle of the Divine. The final transition in consciousness comes with full realization in Malkhut of the reality of our own existence. The human animal echoes the thought of the Divine in Keter, *Eheyeh Asher Eheyeh* – I am that I am. Divine consciousness is now truly manifest upon Earth. The Divine has entered matter. The miracle of incarnation has occurred. And the angels await the outcome with bated breath.

The *Sefer Yetzirah* talks of Yesod 'testing and correcting' designs. Many types of animal could have evolved to self-awareness. *Homo sapiens* made it because we had certain capacities that others lacked – the ability to walk upright, a thumb, vocal cords that could be adapted to speech. Speech was a fundamental transition. Once the first human named her- or himself, the journey back to the Divine was underway. On other planets in our cosmos, the bearers of the Divine spark may look very different from ourselves. The human imagination struggles with this now in the Yesodic dream vision of sci-fi movies. We try to imagine other conscious beings and how they might be. One day, if we do not manage to destroy our planet first, we may get the opportunity to find out.

THE DIVINE IN MALKHUT

The Hebrew Divine names in Malkhut are *Adonai Melekh* – The Lord who is King, and *Adonai ha Aretz* – The Lord of the World. Although we have the titles 'Lord', the Divine, in Malkhut is usually personified as the *Shekhinah*, the female indwelling presence of the Divine. Malkhut is said to have its 'seat' in Binah. This implies there is a strong connection between the Divine in Binah and the Divine in Malkhut. In Binah we think of the Great Mother of the Cosmos, the precursor of form who creates the universe. In Malkhut we think of the Divine Mother on Earth, female counterpart of the Divine in Keter and often spoken of as the Bride. The Divine is found in Kabbalah, not only in Heaven but also on Earth. This is also recognized in other spiritual traditions. Coming from the Hindu tradition, the Tantric worshipper Sir John Woodroffe wrote that:

> *When the Mother seats herself in the heart,*
> *then everything, be it stained or stainless,*
> *becomes but an ornament for Her lotus feet.*
> *'She lives in the bodies of all living creatures*
> *wherein She is present in the form of energy,*
> *even in such lifeless things as rocks and stones.*
> *There is no place in the world where Mahamaya*[2] *is not.'*[3]

The *Sefer Yetzirah* speaks of Malkhut causing an emanation from the 'Prince of Countenances', Tiferet. Malkhut is talked of both as Bride of the Divine Son in Tiferet and Bride of Keter. Malkhut, the Shekhinah, is the Sabbath Queen entering the palace of time on the Friday evening of the Sabbath ritual in the home. Malkhut is invited to the feast as the Bride of Tiferet, the King. The relationship between the Shekhinah and Tiferet reflects the relationship between the Jewish people and the Divine. When the people are in harmony with the Divine, then it is said that Shekhinah dwells on Earth. It is said that those who are humble cause the Shekhinah to dwell upon Earth; those who are haughty defile the Earth and cause Her to depart. The more distant She becomes from us, the more troubled conditions become on Earth.

Earth-based religions of indigenous peoples venerate the realm of Malkhut as the vessel of the Divine. This message is also at the heart of the revival of Goddess traditions and of women's spirituality movements in all the major religions. When we learn to call the Divine She as well as He, then we learn to venerate those aspects of life, which have been associated with the feminine. We venerate the world of Nature, the body, and the emotional realm, and we learn to recognize their importance.

The qualities of Netzah, Yesod and Malkhut in the Western Mystery Tradition were well understood by magician Dion Fortune. This is how she expressed the mystery of immanence, the Divine indwelling in Nature.

The ignorant and impure man gazeth upon the face of Nature,
and it is to him darkness of darkness.
But the initiated and illumined man gazeth thereon
and seeth the features of God.
Be ye far from us, O ye profane,
while we adore God made manifest in Nature.[4]

Imagine a vision of the universe where each particle and molecule is suffused with Divine energy, so that the whole of creation glows with Divine power. Nature mystics, poets, hill walkers, mountaineers, gardeners and all those who spend time outdoors are open to this power. In Nature we see expressed the harmony of creation and, in her wondrous forms, she shows us the infinite possibilities that the Divine has made manifest in the world of matter. It is easy to forget when we live in our urban environments that we are not solely part of the ephemeral world of media, fashion, business, economics and politics. Our home is Nature. If we are cut off from greenness and from the animal kingdom then we feel alienated and alone in the universe, when in truth it is populated with myriad life forms that are our kin.

Malkhut is the everyday world that we perceive through our five senses. Some people are over-immersed in the material world, but many suffer from the opposite problem: they are out of touch with everyday life. Spirituality can be a flight into another reality, an escape from a world with demands too great to bear. When we feel alienated and separate from the everyday world, it is easy to want to find a way out. Spirituality can be just such a refuge. The beauty of Kabbalistic spirituality is that its aim is not just unity with the Divine in the hereafter. It is about learning to contact the Divine in the here and now.

The Divine, which is neither male nor female, performed the first creative act that made the universe. In Binah the potential for form is created. In Malkhut comes its greatest expression – the natural world. From unity comes forth diversity. The seven sefirot below Binah are often associated with the seven days of creation, or stages of development of life on this planet, described in the Biblical book of Genesis. Malkhut can be seen as the end of the sixth day and the beginning of the seventh day of creation, the Sabbath, when the Divine takes Its ease and sees that all It has created is good.[5] The Divine finds Its fullest expression in Nature. It is as though the Divine is seeking to know Itself and must manifest in every conceivable form It can conceive. The outcome is Malkhut, the extraordinary creation that is our physical world. Nature is an incredibly complex interaction of energies that produces a planet that can sustain human life. This is Gaia, the biosphere. Each living entity within Gaia, great or small, is part of an interacting system that creates organic life. When we feel isolated in our own lives, it is important to remember that by our very act of breathing we are transforming the air into forms that can give life to other types of being. Even our deaths, and the return of our bodies or ashes to earth or water, will feed new organisms and bring new life.

PANTHEISM

For some Kabbalists, the Divine is present or immanent in all material creation. For other Kabbalists, the power of the Divine and not the Divine Itself enters into matter. However we see it, we are left with the idea that the manifest universe is a garment of the Divine and if the Divine should withdraw from the universe annihilation would follow. Here Kabbalah is verging on equating the Divine with the Life Force.

The veneration of Malkhut does not need elaborate doctrines and it can be the sefirah of pantheism. For the Pantheist, Goddess or God is a representation of the force of life itself, which is ever becoming and ever evolving. The idea of a spiritual realm outside the manifest universe is seen as unnecessary. Pantheism teaches us to venerate the natural world around us, an attitude that is important when our planet is under environmental threat. Pantheism can also help us understand that the here and now are important. We must not seek to flee this reality for some vague spiritual one and neglect our responsibilities to our fellow beings, other species and the natural world that supports us. The *Rubaiyat of Omar Khayyam* is a famous Persian text that some would describe as pantheist and others as a Sufi work; even though Omar was frowned upon by Sufis of his day. This celebrates the pleasures of the here and now and of sensory existence. This, verse 11, is perhaps the most famous:

> *Here with a loaf of bread beneath the bough,*
> *a flask of wine, a book of verse –*
> *and thou beside me singing in the wilderness;*
> *then wilderness is Paradise enough.*

TITLES AND IMAGES

The magical image of Malkhut is that of a young queen on a throne. Queen is Malkah. Malkhut is also known as Kallah, the Bride. She is Gaia, Mother Earth, and the body of the entire physical universe. She is the inferior mother, a reflection and realization of the superior mother Binah. One of the titles of Binah is Khorsia, the throne. Binah is therefore the throne of Malkhut, the Queen.

Malkhut is the earthly plane, the world of manifestation. Among its titles are 'The Gate', 'The Gate of Tears' and 'The Gate of Death'. The titles connected with death and sorrow link Malkhut to Binah and Binah's spiritual vision – the Vision of Sorrow. Why should Malkhut and Binah be seen in such negative terms? In part this reflects the perspective of mystics who are yearning for union or re-union with the Divine. For them, bodily incarnation separates them from the state of being to which they most aspire. Conversely, death is considered a release and liberation from the body. To see Malkhut and Binah in such negative terms is a reversal of Kabbalistic teaching that the Divine is immanent or indwelling in this world as well as in the realms beyond. Negative attitudes to Malkhut are bound up with negative attitudes to the body, sexuality and the everyday world. It is easy to think that we need to aspire spiritually to some mysterious 'other realm' rather than find spiritual progress through our interaction with others and with the world around us. We need to remind ourselves that the body is holy. In Kabbalah, the Divine is described in anthropomorphic or human terms and it is not seen as incongruous to equate the spirituality of the Divine with a human form, even if we must remember that this is only an image and not the reality.

MALKHUT AND INDIVIDUAL DEVELOPMENT

As we enter mature adulthood, we find that we have come round on a spiral. We are faced again with some of the existential issues that beset our teenage years. What are we doing? Is the life that we are leading satisfactory? We examine the dreams and hopes that we had for the first part of our life against what we have achieved. Sometimes the comparison is disappointing and even if it is not we must face certain realities. Youth is not eternal and goals and ambitions we held for the first part of life may not sustain us through the second. We come to a point of re-evaluation. We must judge our youthful dreams against the reality of Malkhut.

Malkhut is a turning point in our individual development. It is important that we learn to appreciate Malkhut and that we fulfil our worldly responsibilities of learning to support our families and ourselves. Once we have learned these skills and feel on top of them, we may find ourselves facing a new challenge – the mid-life crisis. We look out at the material world that surrounds us and think, 'Is this all that there is? Is there more? Or is life just an endless round of reproduction, life, death and rebirth?' In Binah, we develop the potential for individuality. In Tiferet, we awake to realize that individuality. In Malkhut, we realize the price of that individuality – hence the titles 'Gate of Tears' and 'Gate of Death'. The knowledge of our own existence raises questions about our non-existence. If we can live, we can also cease to live. The created can be uncreated. At the mid-life crisis, we realize that we are no longer young and must come to terms with the inevitability of death. Often at this stage, we must deal with the death of parents or of others close to us. Suddenly the generation above, who acted as a buffer zone between death and us, begins to disappear. We are exposed to our own mortality.

Death arouses much fear, but Kabbalah teaches us that we need not fear. The death of the body is but a step on an evolutionary journey that takes us back to our original source – the Divine. Kabbalah teaches *Gilgul* or reincarnation. Reincarnation is often thought of solely as an Eastern teaching, but this is not the case. Teaching about reincarnation is revealed in one of the main Kabbalistic texts, the *Bahir*, where the teaching is ascribed to Rabbi Akiba. Life in the body is good and is to be enjoyed but each of us is also a spiritual being who existed before this incarnation and who will exist after it. Reincarnation is one of the secret doctrines of Kabbalah.

We are born, die and are born again. Each life is a new learning experience and we bring with us to our new lives wisdom from the lives that have gone before. The self-awareness that we acquire at Malkhut remains with us when we shed our bodies with each incarnation. Each death is like a snake shedding its skin. We emerge renewed for another season of our life cycle. The fact that we take a portion of our consciousness forward into each incarnation is important. It means that humankind is still evolving. The accumulated wisdom of the generations is born in us anew and evolves further. In Kabbalistic tradition, death is not an end but a new beginning. Life is a journey, sometimes joyful, sometimes painful, but essentially we are spiritual travellers journeying to gain the most prized treasures of all – wisdom, inner peace, ecstasy and union with our chosen and preferred. This cannot be attained in one brief lifetime. The Wheel of Rebirth will turn many times before our journey ends.

QUALITIES OF MALKHUT

The virtue of Malkhut is discrimination. Discrimination is the ability to perceive differences. This is essential to our animal selves. We perceive the difference between cold and hot, so we do not put our hands in the fire. We perceive the difference between solid and unsafe surfaces, so we do not fall down holes. We also make more abstract discriminations – between people who wish to help us and those who wish us harm, between people who are interesting and those who will bore the pants off us. These discriminations of heart and head are equally necessary for our survival.

The negative qualities or vices of Malkhut are avarice and inertia. Avarice is greed, something that we can easily fall prey to when it comes to material concerns. Inertia is closely related to the indolence of Yesod. If we think of the qualities of people we consider 'earthy', we find that they can be too disinclined to change and too stable. If we become too absorbed by the world of Malkhut, we are happy to live in the present and need no goals and no sense of where we are going in the future: we do not awaken to Tiferet. The future is important in relation to Malkhut. We can have completely satisfactory material lives, but for humankind this will never be enough. We need something more, even if we do not know what it is. For this we must have the spiritual experience of Malkhut. This will reveal to us where we are going.

SPIRITUAL EXPERIENCE OF MALKHUT

The spiritual experience of Malkhut is the Vision of the Holy Guardian Angel. An important idea in Kabbalah is that each one of us has a guardian angel or guiding spirit who accompanies us through life. What is a Holy Guardian Angel? The Holy Guardian Angel is a spiritual guide who tries to help us and protect us in our Earthly incarnation. Some would see the Holy Guardian Angel as the True Self in Tiferet, whom we first perceive as separate and different from ourselves. Later in our evolutionary journey we may come to realize that the Wise Person whose counsel we seek is an aspect of our own higher consciousness. The Self is who and what we really are, when all the outer veneer of persona and Ego are stripped away. At the level of Malkhut, we do not become at one with the Self, but it is a call from the Self which awakens us in the literal or the symbolic night of unawareness and calls us to the Divine.

Once we have established ourselves on the physical plane and have fulfilled our intellectual, emotional and physiological needs, then a new challenge awaits us. Conversation with the Holy Guardian Angel, or to use more modern language, the Ego's dialogue with the True Self in Tiferet, brings the realization that, in the words of Shakespeare in *Hamlet*, 'There are more things in Heaven and Earth, Horatio, than are dreamt of in your philosophy.'[6] Beyond the material plane is a new spiritual challenge – to return to unity with the Divine. This spiritual quest is important for others as well as for ourselves. Inherent in traditional Kabbalah and in the Western Mystery Tradition is the idea of the *Great Work*. Part of the task of humankind is to rectify the damage and imperfection within creation. Through evolving an advanced state of consciousness, human beings can help heal creation. This is known as *tikkun* or 'restoration'. Another important reason for our individual spiritual evolution is that we are all connected with one another. States of consciousness are 'contagious'. As each person advances, the collective psyche of humankind advances just a fraction. The change is minute, but cumulatively over the millennia the change is great.

To evolve spiritually, we need to establish a dialogue with our True Selves, the inner guide. 'Follow me,' says the voice of the Self and we follow the best and highest part of ourselves, thinking that we are following God. When the link with the Self grows strong, the Self comes and overshadows us, folding us in its wings, and guiding us on our life's journey. We seek to do its will and not the will of the Ego. Then finally, we become the Self and realize that what we saw as Divine was but a way-station on the journey to the true mystery, which is far beyond our everyday minds. It is not our task here to go on that journey. This we must leave for another time and another round of the Spiral Dance, the manifestation and unmanifestation of the Beloved Divine – Blessed Be Its Most Secret and Holy Name.

EXPLORING MALKHUT

EXERCISE 1: LISTENING TO THE VOICE OF THE TRUE SELF

Here is an exercise to help you grow accustomed to listening to the voice of the True Self within you. To hear the voice of the deeper and wiser Self, we need periods of silence, meditation, quiet reflection and contemplation. These are difficult to achieve in our busy everyday lives, but it can be done if we harness some of the powers of the sefirot that we know are latent within us, such as our will. It also depends on our priorities. If we are ready to begin the journey back from Malkhut, then we will have a sense of urgency about spiritual work and we will perform it. If we are not ready, any thought of such a task will trigger the vice of Malkhut, inertia.

Conversation with the Holy Guardian Angel in Tiferet allows us to harness the resources to which Tiferet has access. These include knowledge (Daat), creative vision (Hesed), will and inner strength (Gevurah), and the ability to combine these into goal-directed action (Tiferet). We can use these in Malkhut, the sefirah of everyday reality, to create a balance between the competing demands of our lives. Often psychological and physical ill health are the result of ignoring the needs of one aspect of our being and of sacrificing one part of ourselves to another. The message of Tiferet is evolution through harmony.

This exercise will help you to explore the balance between different aspects of your being as they manifest in Malkhut. For this exercise, you need quiet and privacy. You may want to light a candle and burn some perfumed oil. You will need four pieces of large plain paper and four different-coloured pens – yellow, green, orange and brown. You need to sit on the floor and lay the four pieces of paper out around you, with you in the centre of them.

1. Write a heading on each of the four pieces of paper, using the different-coloured pens. The headings are *Mind* (orange), *Body* (brown), *Emotions* (green) and *Self* (yellow). Sit on the floor and put the paper headed 'Self' in front of you, 'Mind' to your left, 'Emotions'

to your right, and 'Body' behind you to form a cross with you at the centre. Place the pens on top of their respective pieces of paper.

2. The Self is wise, compassionate and non-judgmental. The Self helps us get an overview of our life. To become the Self, we must make a link with Tiferet. Focus for a few minutes on the wise being that lies hidden deep within your psyche. You may find it helpful to imagine being bathed in golden light.

3. Now turn around to face the paper headed 'Body'. It is important for you to move. This works far better than moving the pieces of paper. Ask yourself the following questions:
   • What are my body's strengths?
   • What are its weaknesses?
   • What needs does my body have that have not been met?
   • What steps can my body take to meet those needs?

4. Spend ten minutes thinking about these questions and write notes on your paper about what comes to you.

5. Turn to face your 'Self' paper again. Clear your psyche of the insights from your body and get in touch with your wise compassionate self.

6. Now turn to your right, to the paper headed 'Emotions'. Ask yourself:
   • What are my emotional strengths?
   • What are my emotional weaknesses?
   • What emotional needs do I have that have not been met?
   • What steps can my emotions take to meet those needs?

7. Write your notes. After ten minutes or so, turn to the 'Self' position again and reconnect to your Wise Self.

8. Now turn to the 'Mind' paper and ask yourself:
   • What are the strengths of my mind?
   • What are its weaknesses?
   • What intellectual needs do I have that have not been met?
   • What steps can my mind take to take to meet those needs?

8. Make your notes and then return to your 'Self' position. Now turn to Body, Mind and Emotions in turn. Ask each one, 'Are you satisfied with the place that I give you in my life? If not, is there any one thing you would like me to change so you can play a more harmonious role in my lifestyle?' Listen to each direction in turn until you are sure that you have understood the answers.

9. Finally, turn to face 'Self'. You may have been asked to make some changes. You, at the centre, must consider these requests carefully and realistically. Can you make them? If not, why not? If you can make changes, when will you make them? It is important to be realistic. Often change is more successful in small incremental steps. Record your decisions.

10. When you have reached your decision, stay facing 'Self' and thank Body, Emotions and Mind for their assistance and insights. If you cannot make the changes they request, explain why not. If you can, make it a promise.

Now you have a basis from which to start your spiritual journey homeward.

EXERCISE 2: THE DIVINE IN MALKHUT

This is an exercise to help you contact the Divine Feminine in Malkhut. Here you will be asked to visualize the Divine as Goddess. Write out the instructions or prepare your tape. As with previous exercises, create a dimly-lit, relaxing atmosphere to do your exercise. Allow about 40 minutes. Visualize each stage of the exercise as fully as you can. This is Malkhut – the element of earth – so go slowly.

1. Imagine that it is night. You are standing on thick grass on a sloping hillside. There is a soft gentle breeze with a faint smell of salt upon it. Ahead of you in the distance is a shimmering sea.

2. You turn and see that behind you is the entrance to a cavern. You see there are flickering flames in the darkness and that flaming torches light the cavern. The cavern extends into a long downward-sloping tunnel. You enter the cavern and follow the tunnel. The walls of the tunnel are of rich, dark, black earth. Here and there tree roots protrude into the tunnel walls. There is a smell of rich earthiness.

3. You find that the tunnel is opening out into an underground chamber. It is a temple. In the centre of the temple is a small altar from which rises incense smoke. There is also a vase of orange lilies on the altar. Behind the altar is a carved wooden throne.

4. You hear a ringing sound – a temple gong – and from a small entrance to the right of the temple a veiled woman appears in a long flowing robe of green embroidered with birds and flowers. She sits upon the throne and you know that you are in the presence of Malkah, the Queen. She is a manifestation of the Divine in Malkhut, the enthroned Goddess who from her underworld kingdom rules the world.

5. All is now silent in this Temple. We have returned to one of the qualities of Binah, with which Malkhut is strongly connected. This is the silence of the waiting place of transformation, which some would call the Tomb. This is a ringing silence like the reverberation of the gong, ringing just below your threshold of hearing. The atmosphere of this place seems latent with something holy and special. The throne that you saw as empty in your vision of Binah is now filled. Remembering Binah, say softly or in your mind the chant of Binah, which we have already encountered in Chapter 3.

In the Temple of Silence,
I shall adore you.
I shall cherish you.

In the Temple of Silence,
I shall cherish you,
I shall love you.

In the Temple of Silence,
I shall love you,
I shall worship you.

In the Temple of Silence,
I shall worship you,
I shall adore you.

8. And now we say a hymn of praise to the Divine Feminine in Malkhut:

Blessed be the Great Mother of Heaven and Earth,

Blessed be the stillness of her holy place.
Blessed be the babe who cries to her,
Blessed be the deer who lift their heads for her,
Blessed be the birds who fly the skies for her,
Blessed be the trees that shake and sigh for her,
Blessed be the leaf that falls for her and nourishes the soil.
Blessed be the wave that caresses the shore for her,
Blessed be the sand that succumbs to its embrace,
Blessed be the shell that is cast up for her,
Blessed be She, the Mother of Pearl.
Blessed be the stars which shine like jewels for her,
Blessed be the Moon in which we see her face,
Blessed be my spirit which soars the heights for her,
Blessed be my soul which expands in joy for her,
Blessed be my body, the temple of her being.[7]

9. The enthroned Goddess smiles and acknowledges your greeting.
    Then you sense a new presence in the Temple. You sense that
    someone has entered the Temple behind you. This person places his
    or her hands upon your shoulders. You sense that he or she is taller or
    stronger than you, but this person's touch, although as light as a
    feather, creates a quivering energy within you. You know that you are
    in the presence of a person of power.

10. Now you sense a voice within your head, as though the stranger is
    speaking directly into your mind. 'Watch and wait,' says the voice,
    'and I will come.' You feel the energy of his or her hands pulsating
    into you like a golden fire, and then it fades. It is gone and you are left
    before the throne of the Goddess of Malkhut, who still smiles and has
    seen all that has passed.

When it is right, you will hear the call to reorient your life to the sacred and
the magical while still keeping your feet firmly planted in Malkhut, the right
and proper place for them. Until then, listen and wait. The time will come.

In the Temple of Silence,
I shall adore you.

I shall cherish you.
I shall love you.
I shall worship you,
In the Temple of Silence,
Blessed Be She-He,
Creatrix and Creator of the Universe!

When you are ready record your experiences and return to the everyday world.

Malkhut Kingdom

Titles: Kingdom, Sovereignty, Shekhinah, Inferior Mother, Malkah – the Queen, Kallah – the Bride, Nukvah – the Female Gate, Gate of Death, Gate of Tears
Image: A young queen enthroned

Divine Aspect

Hebrew Divine Names: *Adonai ha Aretz* – Lord of the Land, *Adonai Melekh* – Lord King
Deities in other traditions: Gaia – Greek Goddess of the Earth, Demeter – Greek Mother Goddess, Geb – Egyptian God of land
Spiritual Paths: Nature worship, pantheism

Correspondence in the Physical Universe

In the Cosmos: Earth
Number: 10
Colour: Earth – citrine, russet-red, olive green, black – which are mixed to produce brown

Correspondence in Humankind

Spiritual Experience: Vision of the Holy Guardian Angel
Positive Quality: discrimination
Negative Quality: avarice and inertia
In the human body: anus and feet

Notes

1. Also translated as 'scintillating', 'resplendent' and 'radiant'.

2. The Goddess.

3. Avalon (1918 ed., page 73).

4. Fortune (1976 ed., page 124).

5. Genesis 1:31.

6. *Hamlet*, Act I, scene v.

7. Vivianne Crowley, 1988.

AFTERWORD: DISCOVERING MORE

BOOKS ON KABBALAH

Kabbalah is experiential, but there are many books that can help you find out more. Here are some books you might try.

JEWISH KABBALAH – PRIMARY SOURCES

The three main kabbalistic texts accessible to English readers are the *Bahir*, *Sefer Yetzirah* and *Zohar*.

The books of Rabbi Aryeh Kaplan can be highly recommended. Rabbi Kaplan was the youngest physicist ever employed by the United States government and became editor of *Jewish Life* magazine. He was born in the Bronx (the setting of Chaim Potok's novels – see below), where he studied in yeshivot (religious schools), before continuing his education in Israel. An inspiring man, he died tragically early at 48.

Aryeh Kaplan (1989 ed.) *The Bahir: Illumination*. York Beach: Weiser.
Aryeh Kaplan (1997 ed.) *Sefer Yetzirah: The Book of Creation, In Theory and Practice*. York Beach: Weiser.

The complete edition of the *Zohar* is a mammoth text, but numerous short editions are available that can give a flavour of the work.

Daniel Chanan Matt, ed. (1983) *Zohar: The Book of Enlightenment.* London: SPCK.

Gershom Scholem ed. (1963 ed.) *Zohar – The Book of Splendour: Basic Readings from the Kabbalah*. N.Y.: Schoken Books.

JEWISH KABBALAH – SECONDARY SOURCES

Professor of Jewish Mysticism, Gershom Scholem, was responsible for the revival of academic study of Kabbalah in the twentieth century. He wrote numerous scholarly books. The front cover of Professor Scholem's book *Kabbalah* describes it as 'a definitive history of the evolution, ideas, leading figures and extraordinary influence of Jewish mysticism'. This is a fascinating work for those interested in the history of ideas and can provide an introduction to Professor Scholem's other erudite works.

Gershom Scholem (1978 ed.) *Kabbalah*. New York: Meridian (Penguin Books).

Scholar Dr. Raphael Patai's book had been highly influential in showing how Goddess worship is an integral part of Judaism. It is a wonderful source of information about the Hebrew Goddess and the Goddess in Kabbalah.

Raphael Patai (1990 ed.) *The Hebrew Goddess*. Detroit: Wayne State University Press.

FEMINISM

Jewish feminists have taken a leading role in reawakening us to the importance of the Goddess and the Divine Feminine. Interesting women writers in this field are:

Asphodel Long (1992) *In a Chariot Drawn by Lions: The Search for the Female in Deity*. London: Women's Press.

Rabbi Shoni Labowitz is co-rabbi of the Temple Adath Or in Fort Lauderdale, Florida, and creates healing rituals in the Kabbalistic tradition. There is a strong focus on the body and her re-readings of the Bible are a revelation.

Shoni Labowitz (1998) *God, Sex, Women and the Bible: Discovering our Sensual, Spiritual Selves*. N.Y.: Simon & Schuster.
Judith Plaskow (1990) *Standing again at Sinai: Judaism from a Feminist Perspective*. San Francisco: HarperSanFrancisco.
Melissa Raphael (1999) *Thealogy: Discourse on the Goddess*. Sheffield: Sheffield Academic Press.

Some women have chosen to stay within mainstream Judaism. Others such as the American Witch Miriam Simos, Starhawk, are important influences on Wicca and Pagan Goddess spirituality. This does not mean that they have rejected their Jewish heritage, but that there are now Pagan Jews and what are sometimes called 'Jewitches'.

Starhawk (Miriam Simos) (1999 ed.) *The Spiral Dance: A Rebirth of the Ancient Religion of the Great Goddess*. New York: HarperCollins.
Savina Teubal (1984) *Sarah the Priestess: The First Matriarch of Genesis*. Athens, Ohio: Swallow Press.

WESTERN MYSTERY TRADITION - CLASSIC TEXTS

Dion Fortune was a leading female magus of the Western Mystery Tradition. Her work is now old fashioned, but still an excellent source text for this part of the Kabbalistic tradition.

Dion Fortune (1998 ed.) *The Mystical Qabalah*. London: Society of the Inner Light.

Magician A.E. Waite's work has been used as a source by many later writers. He covers interesting background on the development of Kabbalah.

A.E. Waite, (no publication date) *The Holy Kabbalah*. Secausus, N.J.: Citadel Press.

WESTERN MYSTERY TRADITION – MODERN TEXTS

Weiser has recently reissued Ellen Cannon Reed's book. It is a helpful bridge for those coming from Wicca to Kabbalah.

Ellen Cannon Reed (1997 ed.) *The Witches' Qabalah*. York Beach: Weiser.

Z'ev ben Shimon Halevi (Warren Kenton) is a convert to Judaism who has written numerous books that bridge the gap between Jewish and Western Mystery Tradition Kabbalah. An interesting example is:

Z'ev ben Shimon Halevi (1986) *Kabbalah and Psychology*. Bath: Gateway Books.

Gareth Knight is a Christian Kabbalist. He has written two useful volumes:

Gareth Knight (1965) *A Practical Guide to Qabalistic Symbolism*, vol. 1. Cheltenham: Helios.
Gareth Knight (1972) *A Practical Guide to Qabalistic Symbolism*, vol. 2. Cheltenham: Helios.

Will Parfitt is a therapist trained in the psychosynthesis of Roberto Assagioli and Piero Ferrucci. He has written a number of books on Kabbalah including:

Will Parfitt (1988) *The Living Qabalah*. Shaftesbury, Dorset, and Rockport, Mass.: Element.

INTERESTING BACKGROUND READING

David Bakan (1958) *Sigmund Freud and Jewish Mysticism*. Princeton, N.J.: Van Nostrand.

FICTION

Chaim Potok was ordained as a rabbi and then did PhD research at the University of Pennsylvania. He was also a US army chaplain in Korea. He has written a series of excellent novels about the Brooklyn Hasidic community and the conflicts that can come about from living at the meeting point of different cultures. A good example is:

Chaim Potok (1983 ed.), *The Book of Lights*. London: Penguin.

Charles Williams was a member of the magical order founded by the Kabbalistic writer in the Western Mystery Tradition, A.E. Waite. His novels reflect Kabbalistic themes, albeit from a Christian Protestant perspective.

Charles W. Williams (1965 ed.), *Many Dimensions*. Grand Rapids, MI: Wm. B. Eerdmans Publishing Co. First published 1931.
Charles W. Williams (1981 ed.) *War in Heaven*. Grand Rapids, MI: Wm. B. Eerdmans Publishing Co. First published 1930.

FILM

Director and writer Darren Aronofsky's award-winning film Π (*Pi*) (1998) is available on video and DVD. Hasidic Kabbalists are not shown in a very favourable light but there are some great examples of Gematria in the film. The film is based in New York and tells the story of Max Cohen, a mathematical genius who, with the aid of a homemade computer, attempts to find mathematical patterns in Wall Street stock market movements. This brings him to the attention of two rival groups who want to enlist his services – and who will use force to do so. One group represents the material world – a group of Wall Street traders. The other group are Hasidim who believe he can uncover long-lost mathematical mysteries of the Torah and can reveal the true name of God. The battle is on for Max's mind and soul. This is the ultimate Hodic movie.

Chaim Potok's novel *The Chosen* was made into a 1981 film by director Jeremy Kagan, starring Rod Steiger and Maximilian Schell. This is not currently available on video but may appear on television from time to time. Chaim Potok appears in a small cameo role as a professor.

INTERNET RESOURCES

The mind that appreciates the complexities of Kabbalah tends to be computer literate, so the resources about Kabbalah available on the Worldwide Web are vast. You can use any search engine on the keyword 'Kabbalah' to find a starting point. You can also start with Colin Low's amazingly extensive Kabbalah Links page – which shows true devotion to the Great Work. It has links to major Jewish and Western Mystery Tradition sources on the Web. You will find it on: http://digital-brilliance.com/kab/link.htm

An anonymous translation of Moses Cordovero's (1588) *Tomer Devorah* (Palm Tree of Deborah) is available on: http://digital-brilliance.com/kab/deborah/deborah.htm

Excellent information about novelist Chaim Potok and his work is available on: http://www.lasierra.edu/~ballen/potok/Potok.menu.html

BIBLIOGRAPHY

Arendt, Hannah (1994 ed.) *Eichmann in Jerusalem: A Report on the Banality of Evil*. London: Penguin Books.

Assagioli, Roberto (1974 ed.) *The Act of Will*. Wellingborough: Turnstone Press

Avalon, Arthur (Sir John Woodroffe) (1978 ed.) *Shakti And Shakta*. NY: Dover.

Bakan, David (1958) *Sigmund Freud and Jewish Mysticism*. Princeton, N.J.: Van Nostrand.

Bancroft, Anne (1996) *Women in Search of the Sacred: The spiritual lives of ten remarkable women*. London: Arkana.

Cannon Reed, Ellen (1997 ed.) *The Witches' Qabalah*. York Beach: Weiser.

Cooper, Susan (1984) *The Dark is Rising Sequence*. Harmondsworth: Penguin.

Cordovero, Moses ben Jacob (1588) *Tomer Devorah* (The Palm Tree of Deborah). Venice. An anonymous translation is available at: http://digital-brilliance.com/kab/deborah/deborah.htm

Crowley, Vivianne (1993) 'Women and Power in Modern Paganism' in Puttick, E. and Clarke, P.B., eds., *Women as Teachers and Disciples in Traditional and New Religions*. Lewiston, NY: Edwin Mellen Press.

Crowley, Vivianne (1998) *Principles of Jungian Spirituality*. London: Thorsons.

Ferrucci, Piero (1989 ed.) *What We May Be*, Turnstone Press.

Fortune, Dion (1998 ed.) *The Sea Priestess*. London: Society of the Inner Light.

Fortune, Dion, (1998 ed.) *The Mystical Qabalah*. London: Society of the Inner Light.

Frankl, Viktor E. (1984 ed.) *Man's Search for Meaning: An introduction to logotherapy*. London: Touchstone.

Freud, Sigmund (1910) 'Leonardo da Vinci and a Memory of His Childhood' in *The Standard Edition of the Complete Works of Sigmund Freud* (1953–1974) (24 vols.). London: Hogarth Press and the Institute of Psychoanalysis.

Freud, Sigmund (1927) *The Future of an Illusion*, Penguin Freud Library. London: Penguin Books.

Halevi, Z'ev ben Shimon (1986) *Kabbalah and Psychology*. Bath: Gateway Books.

James, William (1985 ed.) *The Varieties of Religious Experience*. Harvard: Harvard University Press.

Jung, Carl G. (1968 ed.) *The Collected Works of C.G. Jung*, vol. 11, *Psychology and Religion: West and East*. London: Routledge & Kegan Paul.

Jung, Carl G. (1967 ed.) *The Collected Works of C.G. Jung*, vol. 5, *Symbols of Transformation*. London: Routledge & Kegan Paul.

Jung, Carl G. (1995 ed.) *Memories, Dreams and Reflections*. London: Fontana.

Kaplan, Aryeh (1989 ed.) *The Bahir: Illumination*. York Beach: Weiser.

Kaplan, Aryeh (1997 ed.) *Sefer Yetzirah: The Book of Creation, In Theory and Practice*. York Beach: Weiser.

Knight, Gareth (1965) *A Practical Guide to Qabalistic Symbolism*, vol. 1. Cheltenham: Helios.

Knight, Gareth (1972) *A Practical Guide to Qabalistic Symbolism*, vol. 2. Cheltenham: Helios.

Labowitz, Shoni (1998) *God, Sex, Women and the Bible: Discovering our Sensual, Spiritual Selves*. N.Y.: Simon & Schuster.

Long, Asphodel (1992) *In a Chariot Drawn by Lions: The Search for the Female in Deity*. London: Women's Press.

Margliot, Re'uven, (1964 ed.) *Sefer ha-Zohar*. 3 vols. Jerusalem.

Matt, Daniel C., ed., (1983) *Zohar: The Book of Enlightenment*. Mahwah, N.J.: Paulist Press.

McGregor Mathers, S.L. (1991 ed.) *The Qabalah Unveiled*. London: Arkana.

Newman, Barbara, ed., (1987) *Sisters of Wisdom: St Hildegard's Theology of the Feminine*. Berkeley: University of California Press.

Parfitt, Will (1988) *The Living Qabalah*. Shaftesbury, Dorset, and Rockport, Mass.: Element.

Patai, Raphael (1990 ed.) *The Hebrew Goddess*. Detroit: Wayne State University Press.

Plaskow, Judith (1990) *Standing again at Sinai: Judaism from a Feminist Perspective*. N.Y.: HarperCollins.

Poncé, Charles (1974) *Kabbalah: An Introduction and Illumination for the World Today*. London: Garnstone Press.

Potok, Chaim (1983 ed.), *The Book of Lights*. London: Penguin.

Raphael, Melissa (1999) *Thealogy: Discourse on the Goddess*. Sheffield: Sheffield Academic Press.

Rotenberg, Mordechai (1997) *The Yetzer: A Kabbalistic Perspective on Eroticism and Human Sexuality*. Northvale, N.J.: Jason Aronson Inc.

Scholem, Gershom (1976 ed.) *Major Trends in Jewish Mysticism*. N.Y.: Schocken Books.

Scholem, Gershom (1978 ed.) *Kabbalah*. New York: Meridian (Penguin Books).

Scholem, Gershom ed. (1963 ed.) *Zohar – The Book of Splendour: Basic Readings from the Kabblah*. N.Y.: Schocken Books.

Starhawk (Miriam Simos) (1979) *The Spiral Dance: A Rebirth of the Ancient Religion of the Great Goddess*. San Francisco: HarperSanFrancisco.

Teubal, Savina (1984) *Sarah the Priestess: The First Matriarch of Genesis*. Athens, Ohio: Swallow Press.

Waite, Arthur E. (no publication date) *The Holy Kabbalah*. Secausus, N.J.: Citadel Press.

Williams, Charles W. (1965 ed.), *Many Dimensions*. Grand Rapids, MI: Wm. B. Eerdmans Publishing Co.

Williams, Charles W. (1981 ed.) *War in Heaven*. Grand Rapids, MI: Wm. B. Eerdmans Publishing Co.

Wynn Westcott, William (1975 ed.) *Sepher Yetzirah*. York Beach: Weiser.

INDEX

A WOMAN'S KABBALAH